HEARING *is* BELIEVING

Also by Elisa Medhus, M.D.

Raising Children Who Think for Themselves
Raising Everyday Heroes: Parenting Children to Be Self-Reliant

HEARING *is* BELIEVING

How Words Can Make or Break Our Kids

Elisa Medhus, M.D.

New World Library
Novato, California

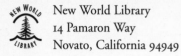

New World Library
14 Pamaron Way
Novato, California 94949

Front cover design by Mary Ann Casler
Text design and typography by Tona Pearce Myers

Library of Congress Cataloging-in-Publication Data
Medhus, Elisa.
  Hearing is believing : how words can make or break our kids / Elisa Medhus.
    p.   cm.
  Includes index.
  ISBN 1-57731-427-1 (pbk. : alk. paper)
  1. Child rearing. 2. Communication in the family. 3. Parent and child.
I. Title.
  HQ769.M38727 2004
  649'.1—dc22   2004002039

First printing, April 2004
ISBN 1-57731-427-1
Printed in Canada on partially recycled, acid-free paper
Distributed to the trade by Publishers Group West

10   9   8   7   6   5   4   3   2   1

In memory of Åslaug Medhus, a.k.a. Bestemor,
11 December 1925 – 13 June 2003,
the quintessential mother who always spoke
a language everyone could understand:
the language of unconditional love.

CONTENTS

Chapter 13
Words from Siblings and Peers   227

FOREWORD *by*
DR. BERNIE SIEGEL

*M*any people do not realize how important the words we choose are to the well-being of our children. Kids who grow up around adults who use communication to foster self-esteem and self-worth are less likely to become addicts or delve into self-destructive behavior, searching for feelings they never felt from their parents, teachers, and clergy. In fact, studies even show they are physically healthier all their lives, too.

Starting in childhood, our connections and relationships are what create our lives and make them meaningful. I come from a minority: those who were loved by their parents, had no problems in school, and got along with God. I respected and loved my parents, and they did the same for their children. Their voices always went with me, and when I made agreements with them, I never broke the faith we shared.

I always tell people if you want to encourage children, say nice things about them to other adults while they are within earshot. How does that help? I can remember as a child hearing my father say, "That boy will be a success no matter what he decides to do." He said that to his friends thinking I was out of the house, so I knew he really meant it. It made me feel very good about myself, much more so than if he had said it to me directly. Elisa Medhus has also discovered this tactic, referring to it as "overheard praise," which she discusses in chapter 7.

Another important point is that criticism can be helpful, but it has to be constructive, nonjudgmental, and given in the way a coach would criticize a performer to improve his performance. If you say, "There is something wrong with you," you are not criticizing the child's actions or skills; you are hurting him. You need to express love to your children even when you might not like their actions, a fact that Elisa Medhus thoroughly explains in this book.

Don't project your faults and problems onto your children. When disputes arise, learn to listen to their criticism and to say, "I'm sorry." After that, healing can occur and relationships can be strengthened. By not making excuses and by accepting responsibility for your actions, you can teach your children to do the same. One way of doing this is to use the pronoun "I" when talking about how you feel, rather than blaming them for what you are experiencing. Then you are not criticizing them but expressing your feelings, and they can respond without feeling blamed. Elisa Medhus refers to this as using "I" statements, and she offers numerous examples to show you how you can adopt this practice yourself.

Here's an example of my own: many years ago when one of our sons was considering buying a motorcycle, I told him about my experience as a surgeon with people who had been in accidents while riding motorcycles. He gave me a hard time, and we debated the topic. I shared from my heart my concerns and how I was sure I would worry each time the phone rang that it might be a call telling me he had been in an accident. After arguing with me and testing me, he went back to his friends, relayed my lecture to them, and told them, "no motorcycles."

My family has learned to use certain sayings to communicate the need for change. When I was acting overpowering, my kids would say, "Dad, you're not in the operating room now." I would always take a step back after that one. Another example is a phrase my wife uses to quiet me down. (I come from a large, loud family, and sometimes my volume is too much for her.) Because we now have a house full of pets, my wife gets me to lower my volume by saying, "Honey, you're frightening the animals."

I also have been known to let my children experience "logical consequences," as Elisa Medhus puts it. For example, when my kids were young I would usually refuse to fix or replace things they had broken when roughhousing or fighting. The kids would have to live without the broken things, and this consequence was another effective communication tool.

Don't ever forget that the opposite of love is not hate but indifference. In communicating with kids, indifference crops up as telling children what to do without listening to what they have to say. I have learned that when I listen to my children share their problems, they always say, "Thanks, Dad, you're a big help." When I instead prescribe advice and don't listen, they say, "You're no help." In listening to children, we give them the opportunity to realize who and where they are and what they need to do.

The key to listening is that it will allow you to understand. And when you understand you can forgive and heal your relationship. When I feel hurt by one of our children I tell them so, and invariably they share what is happening in their life and why they acted as they did. We heal and move on. Remember that the child is a mirror of the parent; what you see in your child that you do not like is what is within you that you do not like.

Today my children are grown, but still they never finish a conversation, in person or over the phone, without saying, "I love you." There is nothing I will ever hear that says as much to me as those three words. Listen to the children in your life, and chances are you will hear those words, too.

When you love your children and speak to them following the guidelines Elisa Medhus offers in this book you will avoid turning them into ugly ducklings who must find their own beauty and re-parent themselves. So listen, believe, and heal.

ACKNOWLEDGMENTS

*T*o every mom or dad who has cringed after uttering words that make them shudder and think, "Help! I'm turning into my parents!" Special thanks to my editors, Georgia Hughes, Kristen Cashman, and Michael Ashby, as well as to Tona Pearce Myers, Mary Ann Casler, and the rest of the team at New World Library who worked tirelessly behind the scenes. Above all, I want to extend my sincerest gratitude (groveling on bended knee, no less) to my five children, who have all shouldered the brunt of the many parenting mistakes I've made over the years — mistakes that have blessed me with a wellspring of material for this book.

INTRODUCTION

i've always taken enormous pride (whether I deserved the credit or not) in being the kind of person who gets things done. Ms. Efficiency. Ms. A-to-B. Ms. Freight Train (don't linger on my tracks, or you'll be flattened). Being a human tornado may work well in some settings, but it wreaks havoc in others. First, it doesn't mesh well with other facets of my personality, like the fondness I feel for my patients. Practicing medicine wouldn't be nearly as rewarding if I couldn't take the time to develop and enjoy my relationships with them. Suppose, in the name of efficiency, I tore into an exam room, thrust a nasty-tasting wooden stick into a patient's mouth, and, after glancing briefly into that abyss with a penlight, announced, "You've got tonsillitis. Take these pills and see me in a week," only to walk out without another word. Sure, it might get the job done, but what about the patient? There she'd sit on the exam table in the jet wash I left behind looking poleaxed. She'd feel confused, even angry. Worse, she'd come away feeling like a number rather than a person with emotions, relationships, and a life history punctuated with happiness and tragedy. So, instead of leaving my office feeling acknowledged as a human being, she'd leave feeling that she was (at least in her doctor's eyes) just another faceless patient with "tonsillitis" stamped on her forehead. Not only would she never return (except to demand a refund and give me a good tongue-lashing), I seriously doubt she'd follow my advice. As for me, medicine would be nothing more than tedious and unfulfilling assembly-line work.

My fondness for people is the main reason I chose to become a physician in the first place. I love spending time with each patient, not only to listen to their problems, share my insights, and help them get well, but also to get to know them as human beings with their own personal stories, families, worries, and dreams. Connecting with my patients makes practicing medicine an immensely rewarding experience for me, and nurturing that doctor-patient relationship has helped me establish a loyal following of patients who consistently take my suggestions seriously. In short, it has become a healing experience for both sides.

But for the first several years practicing medicine, I wrestled with the transition from doctor to mommy, especially whenever I came home to find that my five children had transformed our house into an unsettling mixture of calamity and chaos, more reminiscent of a nuclear test site than a peaceful refuge from a hard day's work. I remember one day in particular: My four-year-old was totally absorbed in plastering panty liners all over the toilet seats — his idea of contributing to the family by keeping everyone's bottom warm. Before he could even explain himself, I let him have it with, "What do you think you're doing? Do you know how hard it's going to be to take those off? Go to your room right now!" No more than five minutes later, my ten-year-old tracked so much mud onto the kitchen floor it looked like he'd just plowed the back forty after a monsoon. Still exasperated by the whole panty-liner fiasco, I hollered, "Stop making a mess! I'm sick and tired of telling you to take your shoes off before you come inside!" While I was mopping up, I overheard my eight-year-old threatening to feed his little sister's Barbie doll to our weimaraner, Zoe, the family's seventy-pound canine garbage disposal. Through gritted teeth and in a tone that might bring certain scenes from *The Exorcist* to mind, I warned him, "If you so much as let Zoe *breathe* on that doll, you're grounded for a year, young man." By then, the first kid was wailing so loudly I started getting visions of my finest crystal shattering from the tsunami of 250,000-decibel sound waves. I hollered up to him, "Don't you make me come up there, or I'll give you a *real* reason to cry!" Meanwhile, my youngest was thoroughly engrossed (couldn't ask for a better word) in one of her favorite tasks: blissfully digging a juicy booger out of her nose. I ran to intercept her before she could spackle the coffee table with it. Little did I know the kids had sprayed furniture polish all over the floor so they could slide around in their socks. So there I was, a human hockey puck, skidding across the hardwood floor in a not-so-ladylike pose screaming, "Quit picking your nose. That's disgusting!"

By the time it was all over, everyone was in tears. My nerves were so frayed the little muscles around my ever-deepening crow's feet were twitching uncontrollably. Worse still, I really hadn't accomplished anything constructive. With the "Calgon, take me away" commercial endlessly replaying itself in the back of my mind, I resigned myself to a long bubble bath so I could contemplate what had just happened. After soaking a few minutes, I began to ask myself, "Why do I treat adults so differently than I do my own children?" What puzzled me even more was that I do so despite the obvious: it never really does any good.

Deep inside, I knew I wasn't alone — there were others out there. As I transformed into a giant prune, ignoring the knocks on the bathroom door, the fingers wiggling beneath it, and the sniveling whimpers in the background, I thought about my neighbors, my friends, strangers in the grocery line with a cartful of toddlers — they all talk to their kids the same way. Then — somewhere between my shampoo and crème rinse — I had an epiphany: throughout history, generation after generation of adults have been communicating with children in a way they would not dare do with other adults. I started to wonder about the effects of our legacy of adult-child communication — other than destroying any hopes of having a peaceful Ozzie and Harriet type family and other than being a highly ineffective way of encouraging obedience. Does it have any impact on children's self-esteem? Is it responsible, at least in part, for some of the problems we see among youth today? And, most important, if adult-child communication has contributed to these problems, will changing it help shape society for the better? All this revelation in the company of disgusting soap scum!

Once I toweled the bubbles off, scraped the panty liners from the toilet seats, mopped the mud from the floors, soothed my five children, and kissed their tears away, I embarked on a mission, a mission to see if there truly *is* a link between how we speak to children and the shape society is in today. To uncover answers to these questions, I conducted hundreds of interviews with parents, teachers, kids, grandparents, and other adults who interact regularly with children. Once I examined the results along with my own personal experiences and reflection, it all became clear: what we say to kids plays a pivotal role in whether they grow to be moral, responsible adults.

In the next chapter, I will explain how, for centuries, parents and other adults have been programmed to make two types of mistakes when they interact with children. The first mistake: some of the phrases we say to them encourage approval seeking. Although it might sound like a dream come true to have a child who will do anything short of throwing rose petals in our path in order to win our approval, that same kid will be seeking someone else's approval later on — someone who might not have the child's best interests at heart as we do, or someone who doesn't share the same principles and values. The second mistake: certain phrases we adults make hinder the development of reasoning skills in kids. Some prevent them from thinking *objectively.* Some make it impossible for them to think *clearly.* And some make it tough for them to think at all! When children don't develop healthy reasoning skills, they rely on others to think for them. Without those skills, they aren't proficient at filtering and interpreting messages from external sources, so they become vulnerable to all sorts of outside influences, positive or negative. And since negative influences often speak to their urges and temptations rather than their morals and values, children who cannot reason effectively can be easily led astray by peer, media, and pop-culture influences that encourage them to make irresponsible, immoral, and perhaps even life-threatening choices.

You may argue that there are plenty of children today who behave responsibly and obediently. But is this merely a reflection of wanting to please adults and other authority figures? Is this their way of avoiding punishment or reprimands? Would they behave that way if no one were watching? In truth, many children make the majority of their moral choices based on their *own* self-indulgent needs and wants fashioned by temptation, spurred by impulse, guided by a thirst for approval, or perhaps a little of each. In other words, they often do the right thing only if one or more of the following three conditions exist:

❖ there's something in it for them;

❖ everyone else is doing it; or

❖ they think they might get caught if they don't do the right thing.

Clear reasoning is essential to making responsible choices that can withstand the relentless lure of outside influences and inner urges; responsible choices impervious to such conditions are the key to being decent, happy, and whole.

As you read, you may be surprised, even shocked, by some of the phrases I list as harmful. (As if anyone with a couple of years' experience taking care of kids can be shocked by anything!) You might think, "I say that all the time, and it doesn't seem to be a big deal. I mean, my kid's not wearing black lipstick and a purple Mohawk. He's not failing school or torturing small animals. In fact, he seems perfectly fine, between the tantrums, the lies, the demands, and the whining typical of childhood and adolescence. What could be so wrong?" But as you read on, you will see just how each phrase alters, distorts, and even hampers a specific part of the child's choice-making process. Since eliminating these phrases may leave many of you with big gaps in your vocabulary, and since filling those gaps with Swahili or Portuguese might not be your idea of an acceptable backup plan, I will suggest a variety of healthier alternatives — phrases that encourage children to think clearly and rationally so they can make responsible choices day after day for the rest of their lives.

By changing the way we communicate with children, we go a step beyond giving them the tools they need to choose wisely. Think about it for a moment. Responsible choices are the individual fibers weaving the moral fabric in a society. Any words that discourage, block, or weaken the reasoning skills of today's youth are irrefutable accomplices in our society's mounting moral bankruptcy. In fact, I believe this "adultese" dialect we have inherited represents the *root cause* of most, if not all, the problems we face today among our youth, our families, our schools, our communities, and our society as a whole. Once we fully expose this connection, we can understand it, and once we understand it, we can divest ourselves of this legacy of harmful words and replace it with another — one that can guide all children to become moral, responsible adults and, as a result, hoist our society back up to its feet. These are the words that will blaze a path to a brighter future for us all.

I

THE EVOLUTION *of*
ADULT-CHILD COMMUNICATION

*t*he relationship between children and adults has changed profoundly over the centuries. Fortunately, most of the changes have been positive. For instance, for several generations, indigent children were exploited as cheap labor — a fact my own kids occasionally try to wield against me at chore time. Their value beyond laborers on farms or in factories was largely unrecognized. Although children from affluent families were spared this abuse, they were still looked upon not as unique individuals but as vessels for the passage of the family name, power, and fortune. Regardless of socioeconomic status, throughout history children have most often been perceived as burdens, necessary evils, and nuisances, tolerated only when they answered an adult's needs or wants.

During the mid-1900s, the parent-child relationship was an autocratic one: the father was the authoritarian dictator and the child, his obedient subject. The mother was the nurturing housekeeper whose jurisdiction in that dictatorship was limited. Aside from vacuuming, baking, and alphabetizing the spice rack, her main function in life was to utter the same two phrases over and over: "Ask your father" and "Wait until your father gets home." Overall, adult-child interaction was based on the philosophy that "children are to be seen and not heard" and characterized mostly by one-way military-style commands and judgments, lengthy lectures, and other didactic explanations that (as agony levels go) rivaled any instrument of torture. My husband is one of the last vestiges of that era. There is some electrical circuit still buried deep in his brain that must have been spared the giant wave of family democratization where, in a mass mutiny, autocrats were ousted from power and replaced with lenient negotiators, ambassadors, and mediators — no sooner does he hear the words, "Papa, can I . . . ?" than he sounds out a knee-jerk "NO!"

During the '70s and '80s, adults focused on pampering the personal needs and dreams that were squelched during their dictatorial upbringing. This self-absorption led some parents to neglect their relationships with their children, ushering in the era of the latchkey child, the "unparented generation." On the one hand, these children weren't subjected to commands and controls, but on the other, they were deprived of the nurturing, support, and guidance so crucial to growing up whole. They may just as well have been raised by wolves.

In the '90s, the adult-child relationship took a turn for the better. Suddenly, society regarded children as the center of the universe, and family took precedence over work. Changing tables popped up in public restrooms — both men's and women's. Family entertainment options sprouted up in every neighborhood. Today, Las Vegas has even blended its sleaze appeal with a Disneyesque tone. This cultural shift from adult- to youth-centric transformed the adult-child relationship from an oppressive dictatorship to a shaky democracy. Now, grown-ups must almost ask permission to discipline children. They vacillate from being the child's manager to a contestant in a popularity contest where the child is the only judge. For the most part, communications are limited to negotiations, pleadings, long-winded explanations, and other futile and exhausting two-way exchanges.

Amid the ever-evolving adult-child relationship, however, the two mistakes I mentioned in the introduction are the constants that have remained steadfast for generations:

❖ We raise children to make their choices based on outside approval.

❖ We hinder the natural development of their reasoning abilities.

These parenting errors have arisen because of the conflict between our pack tendencies and our reasoning abilities. Let me explain:

We are driven by some of the same instincts that shape the behavior of pack animals, such as wolves. Don't panic — I'm not referring to howling at the moon, marking our territory, or rolling around in roadkill. Instead, the common bond we share with pack species is the strong instinctive urge to belong to a group — to feel accepted by others. Indeed, our society is the mother of all packs. We have all sorts of physical and financial standards that make up the general consensus of how success should be defined. Unspoken social mores tell us adults that we stand a better chance of being accepted if we're wealthy, famous, good looking, surrounded by material luxuries, working in a prestigious career, living in a big house, or, ideally, all of the above. If we want to be accepted, we're expected to comply with those standards to the fullest extent possible, and the better we comply, the higher our rank in the pack's pecking order.

Unlike wolves, however, we have reasoning skills. We humans are uniquely placed as the only living creatures capable of using our own free will to decide how to deal with our instincts; we can choose between constructive and destructive ways of doing so. The best way to satisfy the urge to belong is to come up with some unique contribution or carve out some meaningful role that benefits the pack (in our case, society at large) while still honoring our personal moral principles. Those who do this are often rewarded with acceptance. In other words, they become "pack-worthy." Once stamped with the pack's seal of approval, these individuals are free to make choices according to their *own* values and standards, rather than following the pack's without question. They reflect on the pros, cons, alternatives, and potential consequences of each action before deciding what to do. Any negative influences examined through this reasoning process are discarded as useless or harmful. Any positive influences are reflected in choices that add something valuable to their lives. And all this is done under complete, conscious control. The ultimate decision, therefore, is the individual's. People who make choices this way are *self-directed*. They use their own value system as an internal beacon to guide them safely through every influence of the outside world — negative or positive.

Unfortunately, most adults don't fall into this category, but are under the hypnotic spell of the pack's standards and values rather than their own, forever running in life's rat race, pursuing dreams fashioned by others — dreams that are often far beyond their reach. When everyone strives to meet the same expectations instead of creating their own unique niche, we all have to vie for the most favorable spots in the pecking order. Thus, everyone is sorted into two groups: winners and losers. Naturally, many of us would do just about anything to avoid being a loser, even if that means casting aside the values we once treasured in favor of those set by the group. Furthermore, because of this overly focused drive to be better than as many other people as we can, we disregard other essentials that are crucial to making sound choices: lessons learned from past experiences (either others' or our own), our repertoire of strengths and weaknesses, and new ideas born of our own creative thought.

When we rely on the pack to make choices for us, we don't regularly think for ourselves. Over time, our entire reasoning mechanism atrophies from disuse. Without the strong inner compass of our reasoning skills, we easily succumb to temptation and impulse, replacing reason with inner dishonesty tactics like excuses, self-deceit, and rationalizations. Once we abandon clear and conscious thought, we almost *have* to rely on others to think for us. A vicious cycle is born wherein the drive for approval hinders reasoning, and poor reasoning in turn makes us more dependent on the approval-driven choices of others. In this way, we have become a society that is *externally directed.*

Consider the effect this has on children. As neophytes in the quest for pack approval, they're just beginning to find and form bonds. Their identities are in the fragile stages of development. Their capacity for judgment is still emerging. Their system of beliefs and values has barely begun to gel. Cast them into a world where they must follow a set of externally derived standards to fulfill their instinct to belong, and all hell breaks loose. From birth, their choices are increasingly motivated by a desire for approval rather than their sense of right and wrong. At some point, their burgeoning identities, and therefore their self-esteems, risk being hijacked and molded by others, including their parents and siblings, their peers, the media, and popular culture. That's all well and good if the influences shaping them are positive, but what if they're not? In some cases, children are at the mercy of value systems that may not have their best interests at heart. An allegiance to these may require them to make choices that betray their fledgling sense of right and wrong. And to protect their own conscience, they may have to be dishonest with themselves on a regular basis. Over time, they construct an elaborate defense system to help convince themselves that each bad choice they make is really okay — a defense system of denial, self-deceit, excuses, blame-shifting, rationalizations, and other tactics of inner dishonesty. Extenuating circumstances can make any poor decision a permissible exception to the moral rule.

Let's see how this works with a specific example. Suppose Brandon shows up on the first day of middle school wearing his usual garb: his plaid shirt is buttoned all the way up and tucked into gray Sans-a-Belt slacks. Thanks to a summer growth spurt, these now high-water pants reveal his glaringly white crew socks. Finish that off with a pair of Hush Puppies, and you've got yourself a walking bully magnet — a middle-school casualty in the making. Before sixth grade, Brandon has considered himself a well-dressed boy. After all, that's what he's always heard from his parents and grandparents. Now, he's the victim of relentless taunts and jeers. To win back the peer approval he always enjoyed in grade school, he has to follow the fashions of the middle-school crowd. Within a couple of months, he's convinced his parents to revamp his wardrobe with skater shoes, spiked black leather bracelets, long, silver wallet chains hanging down to his knees, saggy pants cut six inches too long, and T-shirts emblazoned with Cold Chamber and Nine Inch Nails logos. He justifies his radical transformation as a product of being older — as casting aside babyish fashions, because, after all, he's grown up now. Although these decisions are not immoral or irresponsible, the point is they really aren't his own.

As you can see, kids, like adults, are subjected to enormous social pressure compelling them to follow certain standards set by peer groups and popular culture — and they are perhaps in an even more precarious position than we adults, as their personal moral principles have not been shaped yet. As we will see, this has far-reaching, often alarming repercussions for our youth and our world. As you read these troublesome findings, take heart in knowing that the power is in the hands of all adults, including you, to turn the tide in a healthier direction — or even to turn things around completely. By tweaking our adult-child communication according to the suggestions throughout this book, we can kick the deeply entrenched habit of fostering approval seeking and hindering reasoning in children. And once we do, we become the first generation of adults to reverse the current trend of crumbling morals and spurious values. What better legacy to pass on to our children, our society, and our future.

2

THE CONSEQUENCES
of EXTERNAL DIRECTION

*W*hat happens to children raised to use approval seeking to guide their choices? What happens when they go into the world without the reasoning skills they need to carefully consider the consequences of those choices? These questions are particularly crucial now, in an age when kids are inundated by more media, peer, and pop-culture influences, through more channels, with greater intensity, and at younger ages than ever before. Thanks to the digital age and the massive globalization it has triggered, unfiltered information flows at scorching speeds from countless sources straight into the ingenuous and unsuspecting minds of today's children and adolescents. When that information comes in the form of harmful messages, the effects can be deep and destructive, taking a toll not only on each child, but also on their families, schools, communities and, ultimately, society, which is victimized by the irresponsible choices these children make. The following are some of the negative repercussions of external direction:

Lower Self-Esteem and Less Self-Confidence

When children seek adult approval, they learn to measure themselves according to the opinions of their parents, teachers, and other adult authority figures rather than objectively assessing themselves. Later, when a peer group becomes their new pack, they rely on peer opinion to figure out what they're worth. Depending on the groups with which children associate — and the amount of teasing that goes on within those groups — peer scrutiny can take a huge toll on their self-esteem and self-confidence.

For example, if a child has a pimple on the tip of his nose, his friends are probably going to point it out to him (as if the half-inch coating of Clearasil cover-up isn't an obvious indication he is already painfully aware of it), and peers who aren't his friends might very well ridicule and taunt him. Whether the teasing is good-natured or not, chances are it makes him feel as though his looks, behavior, and life are being constantly scrutinized under an electron microscope. In many cases, this feeling leads the child to internalize outside opinion, giving rise to an inner judge that shapes his decisions. Once this inner judge is deeply rooted, it's difficult — in fact, nearly impossible — for kids to look upon themselves in an objective light. From there, self-esteem and self-confidence slowly erode.

Fear of Failure

When children see themselves through the eyes of their peers or their inner judge, failure becomes a weapon designed to sabotage their self-worth rather than as a stepping-stone to success, an opportunity to learn something valuable. Think about it: failure is going to frighten only those who fear the ridicule, rejection, criticism, and humiliation from others. And such fear comes about only when kids depend on outside opinion to assess themselves.

During my interviews, I asked hundreds of children this question: "If you were shooting hoops in an empty gym and you missed every shot, how would you feel?" Every child claimed they wouldn't be bothered in the least. Most said they'd just keep shooting until they became bored or ran out of time. But, when I asked them how they would feel if a person were sitting in the bleachers reading a book, they all said they'd be too self-conscious to go on. Their fear of humiliation would be so overwhelming, they wouldn't want to stick their necks out and take the risk of "failure."

In most children, this fear eventually becomes internalized once they've experienced enough rejection, ridicule, criticism, and humiliation. From that point on, the very thought of potential failure — even if it won't be witnessed by others — can paralyze them. In other words, they develop a bad case of "failure-phobia," an affliction responsible for the rising epidemic of underachievement in children today.

Incompetence

Once bitten by the failure-phobia bug, the last thing kids want to do is go out on a limb and risk failing. They seek the comfort and security of standing still instead, avoiding anything that involves taking a positive risk. They shy away from learning new languages, taking on new sports, exploring different hobbies, acquiring new skills, asserting themselves, expressing awkward emotions, or making new friends. Although failure-phobic kids may be willing to take self-destructive risks like driving drunk, piercing their tongues, or experimenting with drugs, they balk at taking chances where the goal is a measurement of their abilities or their worth as human beings.

Whenever children are afraid to explore the unfamiliar, to take on new adventures, to take emotional risks, and to learn something new, they deny themselves the opportunity to develop competence in those areas. The results: learned helplessness, a lack of self-reliance, and a low emotional IQ.

Despite all their unique assets, children from this most recent generation seem more incompetent than kids of previous ones. I hate to make the tired old "when I was your age I walked ten miles to school — uphill, both ways" speech, but because both my parents worked long hours, my three sisters and I were completely responsible for managing all the household chores when we were as young as eight or nine years old. We did all the laundry (we're talking pre–permanent press here, people), cleaned the bathrooms, did the dusting and vacuuming, and even planned and cooked all the meals.

Most kids I know look at a washing machine as though it were a nuclear power plant with a million buttons labeled in Sanskrit — all capable of blowing up a small country with one push. Most of them haven't a clue how to hard-boil an egg. Ask them to diaper the baby, and you'll probably be met with a deer-in-the-headlights look and nervous twitching. Sure, kids today are expert consumers. Sure, they're whizzes at a computer keyboard. But the sad truth is many of today's youth just don't have a lot of the practical life skills they will need to become competent adults.

Dependency

When kids lack important life skills, their journey to independence is obstructed. For their mother and father, parenthood thus becomes a lifelong career rather than the eighteen-year-long shift it's meant to be. For their teachers, the school year turns into thirty-six weeks of hand-holding. For their grandparents, visits become — well, exhausting. Why? Because kids, unable to help themselves, must rely so heavily on adults for help. And when that happens, they become the black hole that sucks the life out of any adult within a ten-mile radius. I can't tell you how many helpless kids have crossed my path. In fact, until I changed the way I communicate with children, sometimes those kids were my own.

For instance, one of my teenagers was having problems with her Internet connection. If you know kids today as well as I do, you understand that for them this means life on earth might as well come to an abrupt and catastrophic end. An impending supernova explosion in our galaxy wouldn't be nearly as disturbing. My daughter came to me with her complaint, obviously bent on having me take over, but since I was busy cooking dinner, I suggested she call technical support for assistance. Panic slowly crept into her expression. "How do I do that?" she asked in a strained voice. "Well, you can probably find the number in your owner's manual," I replied. "Owner's manual to what? My computer? EarthLink?" she asked, panic turned up a notch or two. "Try your wireless card first," I responded, struggling to concentrate on slicing the carrots instead of my fingers. "Where's the manual? What do I say? What if they can't fix the problem?" The questions came in rapid, wide-eyed succession. It was all I could do to keep myself from ripping my apron off and taking care of the problem for her. In the past, I probably would have, but now I've learned that rescuing children only perpetuates their dependency. Besides, no one was in the mood for TV dinners. In the end, she resolved the problem herself and felt pretty darn good about it.

Identity Confusion

When children move toward adolescence, their primary pack changes from family to peers. Just as Brandon did in the previous chapter, they reach a point when they suddenly realize their peers don't always accept the identity they created to win parental approval. They have to start from scratch, working to create a new facade that will satisfy their contemporaries. This identity confusion drives some adolescents to feel resentment and rebel against their parents ("What were you thinking, setting me up for that kind of humiliation? Everything you taught me about myself and the world is being shot down by my peers!"). And when adolescents come to realize that the identity they crafted for their parents' benefit is not who they really are, this rebellion intensifies ("You don't understand me! Get out of my life!"). In my opinion, classic teen rebellion is *not* a natural biological phenomenon. It is a product of children being programmed to tailor their identity to parental expectations and then recognizing it was all a sham.

A few adolescents will adopt extreme identities as part of this rebellion and as a result of their inner identity confusion. They may "go Goth," donning all black clothing, wearing black eye makeup, assuming morose, if not tragic, facial expressions, and painting their nails black and their faces white; they may pierce or tattoo every square inch of their bodies; they may sport spiked dog collars and outlandish clothing. But is this who they truly are, or have they just traded one false identity for another? Some never arrive at their own conclusion about who they really are — even as adults.

Poor Introspection Skills

Perhaps the most important asset for any human being is the ability to reason clearly. But when children are raised in ways that hinder the development of this vital skill, they often have difficulty making decisions, solving their problems, working through interpersonal conflicts, learning from their mistakes, thinking outside the box, and considering the potential consequences of and alternatives for their choices. They lack a reliable conscience — that little inner sentry whose purpose is to monitor for and prevent the use of internal dishonesty tactics like excuses and rationalizations, to help them resist their unhealthy impulses and temptations, and to make them aware of the remorse they would feel if they made a choice that betrayed their own values. Because that inner sentry is so weak in children who are externally directed, they look outside themselves for direction. And the more they do so, the less they exercise their inner sentry. Eventually, the sentry becomes so weak he slips into a coma, one so deep a stampede of rampaging wildebeests couldn't awaken him. When it comes to this point, these sentryless kids rely on the media, their peers, and popular culture to define who they are, to decide their tastes in everything from fashions to music to food, and to determine what opinions and ideas they should espouse. This is not real life — it's life by proxy!

A Sense of Relative Morality

When children switch from following adult expectations and standards to following media, peer, and pop-culture ones, they may for the first time be compelled to make inappropriate choices. Remember, that little inner sentry is in a deep coma; he's not jumping up and down, screaming out possible consequences for every decision, suggesting appropriate alternatives, or convincing the child to make a wiser choice, and he's not guarding against the use of tricks like excuses, blame-shifting, and rationalizations. So, children not only have a lower threshold for making poor choices, but they are also able to shield themselves from the unpleasant feelings of remorse and guilt that those choices can produce. In other words, children today find it easy to act immorally or irresponsibly without so much as batting an eye. Many can't even recognize the impropriety of their actions, and many can't muster even a smidgen of guilt.

Self-directed children, on the other hand, are motivated by what I refer to as "benevolent selfishness." I know some of you may be poised to toss this book into the fireplace as you think, "Is this lady nuts? My kids are plenty selfish enough!" But what I mean by selfishness differs greatly from the definition in *Webster's* dictionary. Like conventional selfishness, benevolent selfishness involves making choices that preserve your own interests, but the difference is that the benevolently selfish refuse to make others sacrifice on their behalf, and they would never intentionally harm someone else physically, emotionally, or mentally. Why? Because it would make them feel rotten about themselves, and *that* is *not* in their best interest. Thus, benevolently selfish individuals make choices based on the good feelings those choices might produce. They can therefore resist any temptations and urges that, if acted upon, might make them feel bad. Practicing benevolent rather than conventional selfishness requires both self-restraint and a keen awareness of inner thoughts and feelings. Even more important, it means not betraying one's values and principles. This requires inner honesty: no excuses, rationalizations, blame-shifting, self-deceit, or denial.

Our objective, then, is to guide children to be benevolently selfish, so that they do the right thing for the right reason — to feel good about themselves — rather than to avoid punishment, disapproval, criticism, ridicule, or rejection.

Morality is now so full of exceptions, contingencies, and extenuating circumstances that children feel free to break the rules when there's something in it for them, when everyone else is doing it, or when the chances of getting caught are slim. Similarly, they often do what they think is right only if it's easy, convenient, and painless for them to do so, or if there aren't any better options to profit from. As you can see, the phenomenon of relative morality has pervaded our youth culture, and its results include racism, gang violence, bullying, terrorism, cynicism, apathy, resentment, revenge, depression, suicide, anxiety, underachievement, substance abuse, eating disorders, failure-phobia, rampant materialism, a hunger for power, impulse control disorders, social assistance abuse, the winner-loser mentality, sexual issues, a lack of responsibility and accountability, a bloated sense of entitlement, and other social ills. All of these are created, at least in part, by the way we communicate with children. Although this may seem like a complex and knotted mess, take heart — since opportunity and disaster are opposite sides of the same coin, we have the potential to radically change the dynamics at play.

For one, we are a generation of adults who care deeply about children and their future. Most of us would sacrifice just about anything for their welfare. Furthermore, because we now understand the root of this mess, we can address it directly with solutions tailored specifically to the problem. For instance, instead of battling school violence by installing metal detectors in high schools, instead of handling the surge in bullying by adopting a zero-tolerance position in schools, instead of dealing with the rise in heroin abuse in affluent suburbia by beefing up drug awareness programs, we can simply communicate with kids in a way that inspires internal rather than external direction. We can communicate with them in a way that discourages approval seeking and helps them develop an inner approval mechanism. We can communicate with them in a way that allows them to define their own identities, that inspires introspection, and that gives them the courage to choose according to what they believe is right rather than what will gain them pack acceptance. We are perhaps the first generation of adults in the position to heal centuries of woe — to build a better future for our children and therefore ensure a brighter future for everyone.

3

WORDS THAT WORK

*b*efore we look at some of the words and phrases that might damage kids, let's arm ourselves with constructive alternatives. The common thread in all healthy forms of adult-child communication involves changing our role from judge, dictator, or manager to just and impartial guide. If we act as children's managers, we have to solve their problems for them. Thus, they're spared any of the discomforts or inconveniences inherent in thinking for themselves, and the burden falls on us to make them as close to society's standards for perfection as possible. In this role, we're not in the bleachers; we're in the middle of the playing field calling the shots and receiving the passes. But how can children learn and grow this way? If we act as dictators or judges, we're the 350-pound linebackers mowing them down every time they run with the ball until they stop trying to peel themselves from the turf. In any of these roles, we're bound to get caught up in emotional adult-child power struggles that leave everyone drained and overwhelmed. In other words, we get blitzed by the entire defense.

As their guides, however, we can sit in the bleachers cheering and coaching. From this objective vantage point, it's easier to see each incident of misbehavior not as a personal vendetta against us but as a golden opportunity for that child to learn a valuable lesson that will help him for the rest of his life. By removing the emotional urgency we feel surrounding children's problems, behavioral or otherwise, we can maintain a sense of calm and patiently stand by as they learn from the logical consequences we allow or deliver. That way, we can be there, not to judge their performance or worth but to love and support them unconditionally along the way.

Although logical consequences should be our principal tools of discipline, nonconfrontational phrases are valuable as well. Whether you're a parent, teacher, babysitter, or another adult who frequently interacts with kids, you can use the phrases in the following seven categories to encourage kids to reflect on their problem behavior, its consequences, strategies to prevent its recurrence, and healthier alternatives.

Limited Choices

Children should have many opportunities to make choices, starting as early as possible. Without that vital practice, how can they grow up to become effective decision makers? And, every time you give a child a choice, you send her the message that you have faith in her ability to make decisions on her own. Providing a limited number of choices is particularly useful as a disciplinary tool; giving children two or three options is akin to calling in the FBI bomb squad to storm in and defuse potentially explosive situations before they escalate. Why? Because by allowing children to have a part of the power they seek, you can avert many a power struggle. Here are three types of limited choices that encourage self-direction:

- ❖ If/then: "Class, if you finish your morning assignment before the end of the period, then we won't have to shorten recess."

- ❖ When/then: "When you comb your hair and get your shoes and jacket on, then we can go to the movie as we planned."

- ❖ This or that: "Time for breakfast, Sweetie. What do you want to eat, cereal or Grandma's famous French toast?"

Two words of caution: First, try to avoid turning these limited choices into bribes or threats, because then the choice becomes an external motivator rather than an internal one that encourages the child to do the right thing for the right reasons. More about this later. Second, make sure you're willing to accept the child's final decision, otherwise the process of making up her mind is more about figuring out what it is *you* really want, not what *she* thinks is a good choice.

Impartial Observations

The primary objective of discipline is not just achieving obedience. It's also about getting children to consider the pros, cons, alternatives, and consequences of their actions. As their guides, we need to eliminate all roadblocks to that reasoning process. Although yellow "crime scene — do not cross" tape and orange and white sawhorses with flashing lights may come to mind, the most stubborn obstacle to getting children to think is their feeling of being judged. Subjective phrases that suggest they're not all we hoped for can provoke a list of negative emotional reactions that rivals the longest of Chinese menus. Sometimes they'll react by launching a verbal counterattack of their own in order to salvage their wounded pride. Or they'll storm off and slam their doors, only to emerge after puberty. Other times they'll sulk and feel rotten about themselves. But the last thing they'll do is reflect on their behavior and come up with ways to correct it.

Impartial observations preclude these typical reactions because children don't feel attacked by them. Instead, they cause children to reflect in a number of ways. Children might respond, for example, by thinking about ways to resist the urge to misbehave. They might seek the motivation to make a positive choice. Or, if they've already made an irresponsible choice, an impartial observation from an adult might lead them to examine the consequences of that choice. In short, impartial observations help children recognize, eliminate, and replace poor behavioral patterns. Here are some examples:

❖ If you catch a teenager blatantly littering, you can say, "Excuse me, young man. I see you dropped your empty cup. There's a trash bin over there." Compare this to: "Do you know littering carries a two-hundred-dollar fine in this state? How rude and thoughtless of you to throw your trash on the sidewalk like that!"

❖ If your own child hasn't fed the dog before school, you can say, "I noticed Peanut hasn't been fed yet, and the school bus comes in ten minutes." This phrase is nonaccusatory; all it does is get the child to reflect on his dillydallying and come up with a solution. Compare this to: "I'm sick and tired of having to remind you to feed the dog every morning. You're so lazy and forgetful. If it weren't for me having to hound you, that dog would wind up skin and bones. Get him fed, or I'm hauling him off to the pound so they can give him to a boy who can take better care of him." This phrase does nothing but create resentment, anxiety, and shame. I can hear those doors slamming already. By the way, if your child slams his door, march up to his room and, without saying a word, remove it from its hinges and store it in the garage. Return it only when you feel he's earned it back.

❖ If your grandchild is squabbling with her younger sibling while they color pictures together, you can say, "It looks like Rachel doesn't like having crayons taken out of her hand." Compare that to: "Megan, quit being so bossy. If you take Rachel's crayons away one more time, I'm taking you home to your mom and dad."

Objective Information

Providing children with objective information is another judgment-free technique that encourages reasoning. Sometimes, all children need is an additional piece of information to begin reflecting on and correcting their behavior. By giving them that information in a kind and impartial way, you are arming them with what they need to analyze their choice internally. This is also a nonjudgmental way to jump-start their thinking engines to remind them about rules they may have forgotten. Here are some examples:

❖ "Feet belong on the floor, not the table."

❖ "In our class, we raise our hands before we speak."

❖ "It's not safe to rollerblade without a helmet."

This technique is also an effective way to reinforce our rules and strengthen the family identity. For instance:

❖ "Our family believes in telling the truth."

❖ "We use words, not teeth, to settle our disagreements."

❖ "In this family, we believe in honoring our commitments."

Thanks to the ingenuity of children, anything can backfire on you from time to time. I remember using this strategy on my ten-year-old while we were driving to the neighborhood swimming pool. He slapped his younger sister for some earth-shattering reason — maybe she made the unforgivable mistake of looking at him, maybe her elbow strayed into his territory, maybe she just had it coming. So I calmly announced, "In our family, we use words, not hitting," whereupon he promptly shouted some obscenities at her that would make Ozzy Osbourne blush. When I fussed at him, he looked completely baffled and, in his most angelic voice, replied, "But I used my words!" I guess you have to spell it out in black and white for some kids.

"I" Messages

When children misbehave, there's nothing that throws a monkey wrench into the cerebral cogwheels as much as focusing on who to blame instead of how to correct the problem. When Tommy has the family cat, Fluffy, by the tail and is poised to pour your bottle of Nair all over its quivering body, it's hard to forgo reactions like, "What the heck do you think you're doing, Mister? You're a very bad boy to scare poor, defenseless little Fluffy like that!" But when we point fingers and assess blame, kids can't resist launching a counterattack, offering excuses and lies (in this case, "it was Fluffy's idea, she made me do it"), or going the self-pity "I'll-run-away-from-home-then-they'll-be-sorry" route. Any discipline that smacks of accusation will prevent children from contemplating and changing their behavior.

One way to avoid phrases that come off as accusations is to use statements that emphasize "I" instead of "you." That way, you focus attention on how the child's misbehavior affects others (in this case, you) rather than focusing on how he's guilty as charged. It's perfectly reasonable for you to express your anger and frustration. After all, letting others know what's bothering us is an important function of communication. But there are ways to do it constructively. For instance, in the case of the Fluffy debacle, you might say, "I feel scared when you treat Fluffy that way. She could be seriously injured," instead of, "I can't leave you alone for one second! Look what you've done to Fluffy. She's a nervous wreck!" Here are other examples:

❖ "I feel upset when people make faces at the meals I cook." (See how I chose to say "people" rather than "you"? This makes the phrase even less confrontational, but your feelings are still expressed.)

❖ "I can't conduct class when you wander around the room without permission. It's hard for me to concentrate, and it makes me think what I have to say isn't valued."

❖ "It hurts my feelings when I'm not acknowledged for the help I give."

Questioning

One of the most important teaching tools for any guide is open-ended questioning. What better opportunity to keep the cobwebs from collecting in every nook and cranny of children's brains than to throw a question their way? And if one question can get the gears to start grinding away up there, imagine what a string of them can do! When you guide kids through a thought process with a series of questions, you're essentially showing them what they could be asking themselves.

Children are so inundated by messages from their environment that they seldom have the time to practice listening to that little inner voice responsible for helping them sort things out and filter right from wrong, genuine from false, desire from need, and so on. At first, kids must learn how to produce healthy internal dialogue, so consider your questioning the crutch they need until that voice becomes loud and clear. Over time, they'll need that crutch less and less until, in the end, they can toss it into the wood bin for kindling. For example:

❖ "What is our rule about borrowing other people's stuff without permission?" (The child answers, acknowledging the rule's existence.) "Why do we have that rule?" (The child answers, reflecting on the reasons for the rule.) "What do you need to do now?" (The child answers, considering how he must correct his behavior and make amends for his lack of consideration.)

As alluded to above, your first question gets the child to recall your rule to ask permission before borrowing things that aren't hers. The second question gets her to reflect on the purpose behind that rule, which requires her to consider the consequences her actions have on others. The last encourages her to find ways to make amends and to come up with strategies that will help prevent her from repeating the same mistake in the future. If you had said something like, "How could you be so sneaky? You know how upset your sister gets when you wear her shoes without permission! You deserve whatever she dishes out to you," then nothing would have been gained but ill feelings.

The Minimalist Approach

Okay, I admit it. I'm one of the most distractible people in the entire universe. Because I'm easily distracted by my own thoughts, I'm often unaware of what's going on around me. Although my children frequently use this to their advantage, it drives my husband nuts. Sometimes I'm so deep in reverie that if one of my kids is calling my name over and over, it doesn't dawn on me that I'm being called until my husband says, "Aren't you going to answer the poor kid?" On the other hand, I sometimes reach the point where I'm not only acutely aware of the kids' annoying behavior, I can't bear another second of it. My biggest pet peeve is when one of my kids comes to my bedside at six o'clock in the morning and calls out, "Mom?" Is this kid double-parked in the twilight zone? Can't he see I'm asleep? Great, now I have to pretend I am. But he still goes on: "Mom? Mom? Mom? Mom?" After I've had enough, I holler, "Go away! Can't you see I'm sleeping?" only to hear him continuing to whisper, "Mom? Mom? Mom?"

Until we reach that breaking point, we often tune out the endless chatter kids are so inclined to engage in. We are, in effect, "child deaf." Well, children are no different. The more we explain, lecture, coax, wheedle, negotiate, beg, plead, threaten, whine, and nag, the less they hear. In other words, they become "parent deaf," "grandparent deaf," "teacher deaf" — essentially "adult deaf." Once our verbal ramblings become exercises in futility, our power to guide children is swiftly snuffed.

The minimalist approach is a highly effective way of preventing "adult deafness" in children. A short phrase, a telling facial expression, or a simple gesture can speak much louder than an endless kid-filibuster. Some examples:

❖ When Nathan throws his wet towel on the floor after coming home from swim practice, you can point to it and say, "Nathan, your towel!"

❖ When Jennifer is socializing with one of her friends instead of paying attention to the morning announcement before class, say her name and press your index finger to your lips as a signal for her to hush.

❖ When your teen has gone far beyond his allotted time watching television, sweep your index finger across your neck — the universal cutoff sign.

❖ When a child says something disrespectful to you, give him your special glare — the one that has a reputation for peeling wallpaper from the walls and bursting anything in its path into a ball of flames.

Humor

Tickling the funny bone is powerful stuff. Maybe it can't bring about world peace or solve child poverty, but it sure can defuse adult-child conflicts before they explode. Although I'm no Jay Leno, I enjoy using this technique with my kids. For instance, if my two boys start picking on one another and I feel World War Three on the verge of erupting, I might play the Don King role by announcing into an invisible microphone, "In this corner, weighing in at forty-two pounds, we have the featherweight champion of the block, Lukas Medhus. His opponent, weighing in at fifty-six pounds, is defending bantam weight champion, Erik Medhus." Then I might feign a few jabs at their stomachs until the giggling starts.

Although you can come up with your own stand-up routines — and they'll probably be leaps and bounds better than mine — I'll give you a few more examples to illustrate this technique further:

❖ If getting them to choose what they want for lunch is a nightmare, play the part of a French waiter and take their order with a goofy accent.

❖ If they're making a mess of the house, tie a sign around your neck that reads: "ON STRIKE. AS AN UNDERPAID CARETAKER, I REFUSE TO PICK UP AFTER ANYONE BUT MYSELF. ALL ITEMS SCATTERED THROUGHOUT THE HOUSE ARE SUBJECT TO CONFISCATION BY DUST BUNNIES OR DEMOLITION BY WAY OF SMELLY HUMAN FEET."

Beware, though: what one child considers grounds for the giggles another may see as mocking. It's important to have good instincts for what will make things worse and what will make things better. If your instincts are good, humor can pay huge dividends, because when tensions are diffused, kids feel more comfortable approaching the source of a problem and coming up with ways to resolve it on their own.

Many of these seven communication techniques can be used interchangeably or in combination to address any incident of misbehavior. So mix them up; vary your act. And when you use one, go back and mentally practice substituting one or more of the other six. When any of these options fail, we can always fall back on one of the others or on natural or logical consequences. For instance, if you question your children and they don't answer you, try giving a limited choice: "When you feel like answering, then you can go play with your friends. Until then, I want you to stay here and think about it." If, after attempting the minimalist approach, your daughter refuses to get off the telephone, remove it from her room or suspend her phone privileges for a day. But take note: there are ways of delivering consequences and there are ways of delivering consequences. If you communicate them to a child in a tone that reflects your anger or disappointment, if you taint your words with criticism, ridicule, or other negative evaluations, or if your delivery has a "let this be a good lesson to you" flavor to it, you're likely to inflame the situation rather than encourage constructive introspection. To avoid this, consequences should be stated in a calm, respectful, and matter-of-fact way.

When delivered in a polite tone of voice, phrases that fall into any of these categories can't be interpreted as a personal attack, so children won't be inclined to retaliate against us or feel bad about themselves. Instead, they feel comfortable reflecting on our words and applying our guidance to their present and future choices.

These phrases are therefore highly effective in bringing about desirable behaviors and extinguishing undesirable ones. More important, they encourage children to become self-directed and to practice benevolent, rather than conventional, selfishness. Though no words pack as effective a punch as the logical or natural consequences children experience for their poor choices, some types of phrases — such as the ones I've outlined above — are much more useful than others.

4

REACTIVE WORDS

*n*ow that we have our peaceful and effective alternatives, let's examine the harmful adult phrases we need to replace and how we can replace them. At the negative end of the spectrum are what I call reactive words. These are phrases that are so deeply engrained in the minds and vocal cords of most adults, they're often uttered automatically, without conscious thought. Take heart in knowing that, as the mother of five children, I have in the past uttered nearly every one of the harmful phrases that follow — countless times. Even now I mess up every once in a while, and one slips out. A disadvantage of being an author of parenting books is that when I do err, my kids never hesitate to remind me, "Gosh, Mom, you need to go read your book again."

I refer to the phrases that follow as "reactive" because they represent a knee-jerk reaction in the adult to something the child has said or done. Oftentimes they are our way of venting frustration, worry, fear, anger, or disappointment. While most of these emotions are the aftermath of butting heads with children, sometimes they have nothing to do with the child's behavior at all, but come instead from stresses in our own lives. In either case, they represent our being overwhelmed by the concern that whatever child we're dealing with may not grow up the way we want, our feeling that his or her main objective is to make our lives a living hell, or our frustration with life in general. But to that child, these words are brick walls that stop them painfully in their tracks. And let's face it: banging one's head into a wall doesn't do much to inspire rational thinking. So, when we build such walls brick by brick with our reactive words, we miss many precious opportunities to use healthier forms of communication that would instead help children *think* about their choices rather than withdraw into a mental cave to brood or lick their wounds.

The purpose of reactive words is twofold: On the one hand, these phrases are designed to produce a counter-reaction in the child to change his noncompliant behavior to obedience — immediately, if not sooner. On the other hand, they act as an emotional cathartic that vents our pent-up frustrations and anger. And although they may serve these two purposes well, they do nothing to raise children who comply with the rules because those rules are reasonable. They do nothing to permanently assuage our aggravation and frustration, because eventually those emotions are replaced with our feelings of guilt. So, although reactive phrases serve their purpose in the moment, after that, they do nothing but harm. In the rest of this chapter, we'll examine different types of reactive words.

Negative Words

I can't think of anything more ubiquitous in adult-child communication than negatives like "stop," "don't," "can't," "quit," and of course the most pervasive of them all, "no." In fact, we say this last one so frequently it's often the first word children learn to say. Oh sure, at first we think it's so cute that we log it in our baby diaries, videotape it thirty-seven times, and dispatch a full-scale report to all relatives coast to coast, the mailman, the milkman, and anyone else who'll listen (even those who won't). But it soon wears thin, and by the time the children are in their teens, it seems the only time they *don't* say "no" is when we really want them to!

Why do we use these words? Because it's easy — in the short term, anyway. Spouting off negatives is a reactive, shoot-from-the-hip tactic that requires no thinking or effort on our part. Besides, it's pretty effective when kids are so small they still actually do what we say; at that point, it works kind of like stopping a riot with a fire hose. But eventually, they wise up and realize we're just blowing smoke. Suddenly, that fire hose becomes as effective as a ten-cent water gun. They've figured out that we're really just armchair disciplinarians, pushovers who have a hard time mustering the energy to grab a beer out of the fridge, let alone reckon with a disobedient child. So, those negatives that once made children freeze in their tracks eventually just annoy and anger them. They become whiny, sulky, defiant, demanding, and manipulative, retaliating with their own "nos," "but why nots?" "I hate yous," "but Dad said it's okays," pleadings, foot stompings, door slammings, and all sorts of gestures and facial expressions that curdle our blood and gray our hair. What's worse, using a lot of negatives when speaking with children conditions us to see them in terms of what they do *wrong* instead of what they do *right*.

I'm not suggesting you strike these words from your vocabulary entirely, but when you can use one of the alternatives listed in chapter 3, do so. For instance:

Instead of, "Tommy, stop skating until you get your elbow pads on!"

❖ try providing objective information: "Skating without elbow pads is not safe."

❖ try a natural consequence: If it's not unsafe, let Tommy fall and scrape his elbows, then say, "Gosh, Tommy, I'm sorry you forgot about our rule to not skate without protective gear." Here, you just express empathy, so Tommy has no reason to get mad and retaliate. He's left to ponder the wisdom of his choice, the consequences his actions brought on, and the reason for having that rule in the first place.

❖ try delivering a logical consequence: "I'm sorry you are choosing to skate without your protective gear on, Tommy. I'm afraid you might hurt yourself, so I want you to go inside until I'm sure you'll make safer choices."

❖ try making an impartial observation: "I see you're skating without your elbow pads, Tommy."

Here's another example. In this case, your child has just asked you for a cookie thirty minutes before dinner:

Instead of, "No, you can't have a cookie! It's suppertime!"

❖ try turning your negative statement into a positive one: "Yes, you can have a cookie after you've eaten supper."

Here's an example teachers might find helpful:

Instead of saying, "Don't forget to put your backpack on the hook,"

❖ try using the minimalist approach: "Lisa, backpack."

❖ try providing objective information: "Backpacks belong on the hook by the door, not in the middle of the classroom floor."

❖ try giving a limited choice: "When you've put your backpack in its proper place, then you can go take our ice cream count to the school office."

If you're an adult responsible for taking care of kids at a day camp, instead of saying, "Stella, don't dawdle. I don't want you to get lost from the rest of the group while we hike,"

❖ try using humor: "And here at the Belmont Stakes, we have thoroughbred Bella Stella pulling up from three furlongs behind in the last lap. Will she beat the odds and pass Easy Breeze, or will she lag behind the stallion, throwing the mare liberation movement into the Dark Ages?"

❖ try making an impartial observation coupled with an "I" message: "Stella, you seem to be lagging behind the group. I'd hate for you to get lost."

If you're a grandfather taking care of your grandkids over the weekend, and they resort to the old "Mom and Dad let us stay up as long as we want" routine, instead of saying, "No. In my house you go to bed when I say,"

❖ try providing objective information: "In our house, you follow our rules. Saturday bedtime for kids is 8:30."

❖ try giving them a limited choice: "You can either abide by our bedtime rules, or I can take you back home to your mom and dad."

In each of these alternatives, rather than attack the child personally, you show her you have faith in her to reflect on her choices and their possible consequences. You *guide* her rather than *command* her. However, when the child has not yet acquired the ability to reason abstractly, you may have to use negatives along with redirection. For instance, when your toddler reaches for an electrical socket, you can firmly say, "Not safe!" pull him gently away, and place him in front of another activity.

Angry Words

Except for those who've had frontal lobotomies or are under heavy sedation, all adults get angry with the children in their lives from time to time. This sometimes leads to yelling, shouting matches, and angry phrases. But expressing anger is not the problem here. As I've said before, we should feel free to let children know when we're angry with them! But there are constructive and destructive ways of doing so. Destructive ways of expressing anger include hurtful phrases like, "You drive me crazy," "I could just strangle you sometimes," and, "I wish you'd never been born!" as well as angry commands like, "Shut up," "Calm down!" "Quit your whining right now!" and, "Straighten up, Mister!"

These are almost always spoken in a loud and punitive tone. They're meant to satisfy our need for revenge or soothe our own hurt feelings rather than solve the problem at hand. In short, angry phrases are reactive rather than deliberate. Do they help? Sure, at first they allow us to vent the bitter feelings that have built up inside us so we feel better, at least temporarily. But eventually, we wind up regretting our words. Unbridled caustic attacks also have the negative effect of inciting children to retaliate with their own hostile phrases, withdraw in fear, or think less of themselves. When they respond in any of these ways, they're certainly not reflecting on their own behavior and ways to correct it!

Do they learn when we vent our anger at them? Of course they do: they learn to avoid our wrath at all costs — by being sneakier, lying, pelting us with rationalizations for their misbehavior, and so on. However, these ploys foster external direction, because children must analyze external cues like our mood, the recent events of our day, the way we're treating other people, our level of awareness, and our facial expression to determine what they can get away with.

Constructive ways of expressing anger have a purpose: to let children know that what they're doing is bothering us. One of my favorite ways of accomplishing this is with the "four-step approach":

1. **State your anger.** It's okay to do this in a louder than normal voice, but not in a screaming, vindictive, or disparaging tone.
   "I'm very angry with you right now!"

2. **State why you're angry.** Try to include one of the two root emotions behind the anger: hurt or fear.
   "I am upset that you walked all over my freshly mopped floor with your muddy boots. You don't seem to care about how hard I worked to clean house today."

3. **State your expectations for them.**
   "I don't want you to do that anymore. And I want you to find a way to clean up this mess for me."

4. **Request an acknowledgment.**
   "Is that clear?" or, "Will you agree to that?"

The techniques suggested in chapter 3 can also replace destructive expressions of anger. For instance:

Instead of saying, "Shut up!" when a child interrupts,

❖ try using an "I" message: "I can't listen and talk at the same time."

❖ try delivering a logical consequence: "You will need to leave the room until I am finished talking to Aunt Sally. I can't concentrate on our conversation when you interrupt."

❖ try the minimalist approach: Put your index finger to your lips and firmly say, "I'm talking."

❖ try making an impartial observation: "I see you're interrupting again."

If you're a den mother for a Boy Scout troop and one of the boys is disrupting the rest of the group during a trip to the natural science museum,

❖ try using a limited choice: "Jonathan, when you decide to calm down, then all of us can continue our tour."

❖ try a logical consequence: "No one can get the full benefit of this field trip when you're acting up like this, Jonathan. I'll have to talk with your parents when they come to pick you up."

❖ try questioning: "Jonathan, how are Boy Scouts supposed to behave in public?" (When Jonathan answers, he must recall the rules of behavior set by his troop.) "Why do you think we have that code of behavior?" (Jonathan answers, reflecting on the purpose behind those rules.) "What do you need to do to make it up to the tour guide and your fellow scouts?" (Jonathan answers, considering ways he might make amends.)

Again, rather than reacting against children in exasperation, these alternatives allow us to use anger as a tool to help communicate our feelings. They also help kids reflect on the effects their choices have on others, on ways to make a better choice in the future, and on how to make amends for their misbehavior. So in effect, emotions become a valuable tool for guidance.

Time-Crunch Words

Life is on fast-forward for most of us. You can see signs of the hurried life we lead everywhere. Even the names of consumer products hint at this ever-growing condition. One brand of razor blades is named not to indicate how closely they shave but to describe how fast they work. So, I suppose if I use Gillette Mach 3 Turbo blades, I'll have two to three seconds to spare. Hmmh... what to do with all that idle time?

Despite all the conveniences intended to make household and personal tasks easier and quicker, it still seems like there isn't enough time in the day to do the things we need to do. And we pass this perception along to children. For instance, one phrase I personally have a habit of overusing is "Hurry up!" But back when my dialogue was littered with it 247,900 times a day, I could see the frenzied looks in my kids' eyes — a look I put there. They'd get stressed and angry, and then the entire household would plummet into an abyss of animosity and mayhem that would take days of intense meditation and aromatherapy to mend. In my attempts to light a fire under them, all I accomplished was fraying everyone's nerves, including my own, and bringing my own timetable to a grinding halt. So those two words defeated their purpose with astonishing predictability.

Life is so hurried now, our days so jam-packed with countless obligations, that avoiding this and similar time-crunch phrases seems next to impossible. I *still* struggle in this area, but I'm proud to report that I've got the count down to 3,760 times a day! How did I come to my senses? The following personal anecdote tells the story.

A few years back, I had five kids going to five different schools, some of them pretty far from the others. It would have been manageable if my two boys hadn't loved pestering each other at breakfast — and I mean over some critical, life-and-death grievances like, "I had that cereal box first!" "Stop looking at me!" "Mom, Lukas is touching my elbow!" and "It's my turn to have the blue cup!" The only reason all my kids ever got to school on time (usually by the skin of their teeth) is because of my frantic attempts to get them into gear: "Hurry up! We're going to be late!" "Quick, stop complaining and finish breakfast!" "Stop dawdling!"

"I don't have time for this!" Of course, watching Mom froth at the mouth, clapping her hands together wildly, dancing up and down like a ferret in heat, and spouting a litany of desperate threats was, without a doubt, the best entertainment for miles. I sure gave Nickelodeon a run for its money. But, it didn't help. They just got upset with me for pressuring them when their brain cells hadn't yet had a chance to yawn and stretch. Nine times out of ten, they felt rushed to the point of tears. Needless to say, they spent more time complaining about their feelings than getting down to the business of completing their morning routine. But one day, as if hit by a lightning bolt, I realized my usual routine wasn't working. (Admittedly, this realization was no miracle.)

Why were my tactics falling short of their objective? *I was making my kids' problem more important to me than to them.* So one morning I announced: "At 7:15, I'm leaving with whoever is in the car." And I did just that. (I'm sure it will come as no big surprise to most of you that the two boys were not in the car.) I drove off with their three sisters, leaving them behind in the care of my not-so-thrilled husband. When I returned, they were standing in the garage, hair combed, teeth brushed, and backpacks on, with their jaws dropped down to their knees! They couldn't believe I had left them! When they protested, I told them I wasn't the one getting a tardy, and that it was their responsibility, not mine, to get ready for school in time. I also said I had faith in them to make a better choice next time or deal with the consequences if they didn't. They *did* get tardies that morning. In fact (just between you and me), I called the school office on my way home to alert them to the situation: "Evil mother alert! Please be sure to make a big deal out of Erik and Lukas getting tardies instead of letting it slide. I'm trying to teach them a valuable lesson." The school secretary played along. She told me later that she gave them her most astonished look and said, "Lukas, Erik, you're not tardy, are you?"

To avoid time-crunch phrases, we must never make solving their dawdling problems more important to us than to them. When we do, we feel frantic and upset, and so do children. And when their energies are focused on mounting an offensive against annoying adults or feeling embarrassed about being slower than a cross between a slug and a tortoise, they're not thinking about how to solve their own problems. Furthermore, kids are quick to use our feelings of urgency to manipulate us into solving those problems for them. Most important, phrases like these send them the message that we don't have faith in them to conquer challenges, handle consequences, and overcome adversity on their own.

We also have to step back and ask ourselves: will this really matter a hundred years, much less twenty-four hours from now? So we're five minutes late to softball practice. Are all the pressure tactics and complaining really worth the friction and hurt feelings? Or can these situations be turned into an opportunity to learn something valuable? We've seen one example of how a logical consequence can replace time-crunch phrases. Now let's look at other alternatives:

Instead of saying, "Hurry up! We don't have all day!" when your child dawdles in the store,

❖ try using an "I" message: "I hope we're not late visiting Aunt Pauline. I hate to keep her waiting. She might worry."

❖ try making an impartial observation: "I see you're falling behind a little."

❖ try providing objective information: "It's not safe to lag behind me in a public place."

❖ try giving a limited choice: "You can keep up with me so we can still make that one o'clock movie, or we can see it another time."

If you're a teacher and one of your students takes much too long to finish her lunch every day,

❖ try using humor: "And the race is on! Will Andrea Andretti finish her lunch before the bell sounds? Stay tuned for finish-line action after these messages from our sponsors."

❖ try the minimalist approach: Call out her name and tap on your watch.

❖ try questioning: "Andrea, why is it important to finish your lunch before the bell rings rather than spending the time socializing with Emma?" (Andrea answers, considering the rationale for finishing lunch before the lunch period ends.) "What happens when the bell rings, and you haven't had a chance to finish?" (Andrea answers, reflecting on how not having enough time to eat might affect her.) "What strategies can you come up with to help yourself focus on finishing lunch while still enjoying time with your friends?" (Andrea answers, coming up with ways to avoid getting distracted from finishing her lunch in time.)

See how these alternatives don't attack children's sense of worth? Since they're impartial, nonaccusatory, and nonjudgmental, they feel comfortable reflecting on and solving their own problems. Furthermore, when we're armed with responses like these that aren't voiced in apprehension, anger, frustration, or other negative reactions, we develop a sense of calm ourselves. Instead of using a whirlwind of emotions to guide children, we're using our controlled and collected voice of reason. Remember, whirlwinds, like tornados and dust devils, scatter things in disarray. Reason, however, is the light that illuminates the dark — the beacon that guides them through the confusion of childhood.

5

JUDGMENTAL WORDS

*W*hen subjected to judgments — positive or negative — children tend to respond like circus animals. Like the lions, they do what they must to avoid the lion tamer's whip. Like the seals, they perform in whatever way necessary to get a herring tossed their way. Although this might make life easier for any adult who interacts with children, it encourages kids to become approval seekers throughout their lives, it thwarts their ability to assess themselves objectively, and, when this evaluation process becomes internalized, it creates that inner judge that makes them self-conscious about everything from their appearance to their actions and opinions. The stronger that inner judge, the weaker their self-esteem. Kids need guides, not Judge Judys. They need adults in their lives who are willing to give objective feedback, encouragement, and unconditional love, not a row of Olympic judges holding up scorecards. Let's first take a look at various phrases that express negative judgments and then those that constitute subjective affirmations.

Negative Judgments

Criticism, Nagging, and Reprimands

Criticism, nagging, and reprimands are all personal evaluations meant to cast judgment, although they differ from one another in subtle ways. Criticism consists of finding fault in someone. To children, it's a way of saying, "You're on the wrong path to forming an identity that I find acceptable, that I can approve of." Some examples follow:

❖ "Your hair really looks like a rat's nest today."

❖ "Your table manners are awful."

❖ "Getting a little pudgy, aren't you?"

❖ "Tommy, your desk looks like ground zero for an earthquake."

Nagging is just criticism thinly disguised and tainted with passive-aggressive undertones. I used to rely heavily on this ploy myself, because with it I could postpone the inconvenient and often unsavory task of getting my kids to comply with my requests. To me, running off at the mouth was a lot easier than actually getting my kids to clean their rooms. It took many years of motherhood and a couple rooms that would have qualified for condemnation by the Housing Authority before I realized that nagging is like getting on a Ferris wheel that never stops. Everyone on it just gets dizzy and bored. Although most adults know nagging like the backs of their hands, here are some examples for those who don't:

❖ "I don't know how many times I have to tell you to clean your room."

❖ "Honey, I tell you time and time again, you need to eat more sensibly."

❖ "How many times do I have to tell you to sharpen your pencil before class begins?!"

Reprimands are criticism taken one step further. Whereas criticism is an announcement to children that they've strayed off the course we've set for them, a reprimand is the conclusion that they've already arrived at the wrong destination. Reprimands reflect our disappointment, frustration, and anger, or all three. Examples include:

❖ "You haven't even started the research for your book report? I hope you know it's due first thing tomorrow. I can't believe how lazy you are!"

❖ "This is the third time this week you've forgotten to return your library book. You're hopeless!"

❖ "Oh, no! You've broken my favorite picture frame! I can't let you come visit anymore if you're going to be so clumsy and reckless in my house!"

❖ When, for example, the child drops a big juicy meatball onto his favorite pair of pants during supper: "Serves you right. You shouldn't eat like such a pig!"

All of these phrases help shape children's concepts of themselves, sometimes inflicting deep wounds in their self-esteem. We must remember that it is not only unnecessary to judge them but also completely counterproductive, leaving children dejected, angry, and uncertain of their own worth as human beings. Suffering negative judgments is painful. In response to that pain, children strike back at us, mentally cower and hide from our caustic phrases, or rationalize them away. They never (and I mean *never*) see them as valuable words of guidance. Let's look at some alternatives for several of the examples mentioned:

Instead of saying, "Your hair really looks like a rat's nest today,"

❖ try making an impartial observation: "Let's see, you've eaten breakfast and brushed your teeth, so it looks like all that's left for you to do before the bus comes is run a comb through your hair."

❖ try using natural consequences: when a family of crows takes up residence in her unruly mane, she'll understand what she needs to do.

Instead of saying, "Your table manners are awful,"

❖ try providing objective information: "Our family believes in using proper table manners. Making loud slurping noises at dinner shows a lack of consideration for others." (Again, see how I can use objective information to reinforce family rules and values as well as create a sense of family unity and identity?)

❖ try using an "I" message: "I get annoyed by the sound of slurping."

Instead of saying, "I don't know how many times I have to tell you to clean your room,"

❖ try delivering a logical consequence: Although every family has different tolerances for the state of chaos in their children's rooms, my kids must clean theirs every Sunday as one of their chores. At the end of the day, I announce that it's cleanup time, set the timer to thirty minutes, and, when the timer goes off, I come in with a large plastic trash bag to pick up anything not put in its proper place. Everything in the bag gets donated to charity or gets tossed. The reasoning I use: I don't want to hurt myself stepping on all the clutter. And if they

can't put everything away in half an hour, they simply have
way too much stuff.

❖ try the minimalist approach: "Teri, room!"

❖ try questioning: "What is the rule about keeping our bedrooms clean?" (The child answers, acknowledging the existence of the rule.) "Why do we have that rule?" (The child
answers, reflecting on the logic behind the rule and the consequences of not following it.) "Good. What do you need to
do now?" (The child answers, reflecting on solutions to make
amends and avoid making the same mistake in the future.)

Instead of saying, "This is the third time this week you've forgotten to return your library book. You're hopeless!"

❖ try making an impartial observation: "I see you haven't
returned your library book yet."

❖ try allowing a natural consequence: Make sure *they* pay the
library fines incurred, even if they have to earn the money
themselves. Be sure to give them a time frame within which
to pay off their fines.

❖ try delivering a logical consequence: "I'm going to have to take
your library card away from you until you show me you're
responsible enough to return your library books on time."

❖ try questioning: "What can happen if you continue to forget
to return your library book?" (The child answers, reflecting on
the consequences of his oversight.) "Why is it important to
turn them in on time?" (The child answers, acknowledging
the rationale for respecting the library's due dates.) "What can
you do to help yourself remember when the books are due?"
(The child answers, reflecting on ways to avoid forgetting to
turn in his library books on time.)

Instead of saying, "Oh, no! You've broken my favorite picture frame! I can't let you come visit anymore if you're going to be so clumsy and reckless in my house!"

❖ try making an impartial observation and follow up with a logical consequence: "I see you've broken my picture frame playing ball inside. Go get your allowance and I'll drive you to Wal-Mart so you can buy another one to replace it."

❖ try questioning: "What is Grandma's rule about playing ball in the house?" (The child answers, acknowledging the existence of the rule.) "Why do you think that rule is important?" (The child answers, reflecting on the reasons that rule exists.) "What do you think you should do to make things right?" (The child answers, considering ways to pay for his mistake and make amends to Grandma.)

Instead of saying, "Tommy, your desk looks like ground zero for an earthquake,"

❖ try giving him limited choices: "When you've cleared all those papers from your desk, then I can give you the assignment I'm passing out to the class."

❖ try using impartial observations and offering assistance and suggestions: "Tommy, I notice you have trouble keeping your desk in order. It seems to make it tough to find the papers and other materials you need during class. Perhaps we can sit together at recess and come up with a plan to help you organize things so they'll be easily accessible to you."

❖ try using an "I" message: "When your desk is so disorderly, it makes me feel you don't take school seriously."

Instead of saying, "How many times do I have to tell you to sharpen your pencil before class begins?!"

❖ try the minimalist approach: point to the sharpener and say, "Sarah, pencil."

❖ try allowing a natural consequence: Have her write with her dull pencil until class break.

❖ try providing objective information: "It's important that every student start the day with a sharpened pencil. When someone gets up to sharpen theirs during a test or while I'm talking, it's disruptive to me and the other students."

Instead of saying, "Serves you right. You shouldn't eat like such a pig,"

❖ try giving a logical consequence: "You're going to have to get up from the table right now and wash that spot so your pants won't have a stain."

❖ try providing objective information: "It's really easy to spill when you eat in a hurry."

❖ try giving a limited choice: "When do you want to wash those, now or after you've cleared the table?"

As you can see, these alternatives not only help us avoid the adult-child struggles that are often the bane of our existence, but they also help children *think* their way to better choices instead of developing ill feelings toward themselves or us.

Negative Comparisons

We naturally perceive the differences in strengths and weaknesses between children and their siblings or friends. But we're also keenly aware of the competitive drive that spurs children to want to be better than other kids or to at least not be the laughingstock of the bunch. So it makes sense that we use comparisons to capitalize on this competitive spirit. After all, by motivating them to match or beat the performance of those we hold in higher regard in general or in a given area, we stand a better chance of getting kids to do what we want. More often than not, however, it backfires on us. When children are compared to others, they usually get infuriated with us or the competition. Sometimes comparisons mislead kids into believing we find them unacceptable, and they can wind up thinking less of themselves. The fallout we have to deal with afterward includes intense sibling or peer rivalry, children who defy and disobey us, and children who feel they have to constantly measure their performance against others as they struggle with their own sense of worth. Let's look at some examples and their alternatives:

Instead of saying, "Why can't you make good grades like your brother?"

❖ tackle the problem directly, without attaching your opinion of any other person's performance. In this case, you might want to make sure the child understands the whole multiple intelligence concept — that while some people excel in science or math, others may excel in art; some may be geniuses in interpersonal relationships, others may be whizzes in music, languages, and so on. Also, make sure that the child receives the help he or she needs from you, the school, a tutor, or some other resource.

❖ if there is no underlying learning disability or other factor obstructing his academic progress, try delivering an impartial observation combined with a logical consequence: "It looks like you've not done your best in math this six weeks. Instead of rushing out to play after you finish your homework, you need to sit down with me to practice some of the problems you've been struggling with, at least until you seem to be able to handle things well on your own."

❖ try an impartial observation combined with questioning: "You seem to have trouble in science lately. Do you have any idea why?" (The child answers, reflecting on the source of his struggles with that class.) "What can I do to help?" (This question tells the child your role is not to criticize but to help. In other words, it shows him that you're on his side.) "What do you plan to do to take care of this problem?" (This question not only gets the child to contemplate possible solutions, it suggests you have faith in him to manage his problems, even if part of that plan is to solicit your suggestions.) "What do you think could happen if things go on this way?" (The child answers, reflecting on the repercussions of ignoring the problem.)

Instead of saying, "I don't understand why you talk back to me all the time. Your sister never gave me this much trouble,"

❖ try providing objective information followed by a logical consequence: "It's rude to say hurtful things. You need to leave the room until you feel you can treat me with more respect."

❖ try the minimalist approach: Give her your best evil eye.

❖ try using an "I" message: "It hurts my feelings when you say things like that to me. I expect you to be more respectful. Can you agree to try?"

Instead of saying, "You've fallen to the third quarter in class rank. That means half of the junior class is doing better than you. Are you sure you're doing your best?"

❖ try providing impartial observations followed by an offer to help: "I notice your class rank has slipped a bit. If you'd like,

I can help you with your toughest subjects until you feel you have things under control."

❖ try delivering a logical consequence: "Ever since you started going out with friends on school nights, your grades have slipped. Until further notice, socializing will be limited to weekends and holidays."

❖ try open-ended questioning to help determine, for both you and your child, the root of his academic problems: "I see you're really struggling in school this semester. What's different now compared to last semester?" (The teen answers, reflecting on changes that could be responsible for his slipping grades, such as additional extracurricular activities: a new after-school obligation, a more active social life, and so on.) "What goals do you intend to set for yourself for the rest of the year?" (When you ask this question, it prompts the teen to examine his situation and determine if the path he's on will lead him to where he wants to be.) "How do you plan to bring your grades up?" (This question prompts the teen to consider the steps he might need to take to turn things around, and it shows him you have faith in him to figure out those steps with or without assistance.) "What can I do to help you stick to that plan and meet your goals?" (This question tells the teen you're there to help, not criticize. In other words, you're an ally, not an enemy.)

Negative Labels and Generalizations

When children show a persistent pattern of behavior that we don't like, we often label them with not-so-flattering nouns or adjectives. We do this out of frustration and our own sense of hopelessness that they will ever break free of the pattern. But nothing, short of the annoying tape on the side of unopened CD cases, could stick to a child more. Examples of labels include "You're so lazy!" and, "You can't help it, Sweetie. You've always been a slow reader." Hearing such labels, children think of themselves in the terms upon which we've decided: "My mom and dad have me all figured out, so why bother trying to change?" It makes no difference whether our accusations are accurate, because, since children perceive us as bigger and wiser, they assume we know them better than they know themselves. So, they fall for our opinions every time. These phrases could also become fodder for future excuses and justifications. "So, I'm lazy. I guess I was born that way. What you see is what you get. I just can't help it, so why should I bother trying?"

Generalizations are phrases that usually contain the words "never" or "always." Examples include:

❖ "You never remember to do your chores."

❖ "You always forget to write down your homework assignment!"

❖ "You never seem to get anything right."

❖ "You always dawdle."

Sure, there'll be the occasional smart aleck who comes back with, "Hey, wait a minute. What about that time in 1997 when I did something right?" Actually, this is the kind of kid that understands that generalizations are just gross exaggerations of the truth. But to most children these absolutes seem so sweeping that they give up all hope of shaking whatever assessment we have of them. In short, both labeling and generalizations deter children from figuring out who they are, because they assume the job has already been done for them. Let's look at some examples of both labeling and generalizations, along with their alternatives:

Instead of saying, "You're so clumsy,"

❖ try making an impartial observation: Point out what they did *right* in the task, if possible, "Wow, you got the milk out of the fridge all by yourself!"

❖ try making an impartial observation followed by questioning: "I see you spilled the milk. What do you need to do now?"

❖ try providing objective information: "It helps to hold the cup with one hand while you pour. That way, the cup won't tip over."

Instead of saying, "You never remember to do your chores,"

❖ try questioning: "What is our rule about doing our chores before going out to play?" (The child answers, acknowledging the existence of the rule.) "Why do we have that rule?" (The child answers, reflecting on the logic behind the rule and the consequences of not following it.) "Good. What do you need to do now?" (The child answers, reflecting on solutions to make amends and avoid making the same mistake in the future.)

❖ try making an impartial observation: "I see the trash hasn't been taken out yet." You can also say, "I see you haven't taken the trash out yet," but in the first example, the child is less likely to perceive your statement as accusatory.

❖ try delivering a logical consequence: "I heard the garbage truck coming, so I had to take out the trash for you. Since my time is just as valuable as yours, I took ten bucks from your allowance."

Instead of saying, "You always turn your work in late,"

❖ try delivering a logical consequence: "You're going to have to finish your work during recess."

- ❖ try providing objective information: "Schoolwork needs to be turned in on time."

- ❖ try giving a limited choice: "If you can't figure out a way to get your work turned in on time, I'll have to set up a conference with your mom so we can discuss how best to help you."

Negative labels and generalizations are products of our frustration that attack children rather than address their behavior, as the alternatives listed above do. When children feel attacked, they don't stop to think about how to handle the problems they're creating for themselves and others. Because they assume we have that all figured out for them, they tend to neglect determining, for themselves, who they are and who they want to become. Eventually, they can thus come to depend so heavily on the opinions others have of them that they become deeply confused about their true identity.

Guilt, Shame, and Martyrdom

Guilt, shame, and martyrdom are three gems that represent stealthier ways of letting children know they aren't turning out the way we want. These types of judgmental phrases place conditions on what children must do to win our love and approval, suggesting that if they meet these conditions they'll have better odds of living up to our expectations. Phrases that provoke feelings of guilt tell children they've hurt us — the people who gave them life, who feed, clothe, and shelter them, who love and nurture them day in and day out. They're designed to make kids feel bad enough to go through flaming hoops to undo the damage they've caused. With phrases that evoke shame, we express what disappointments they've become, pointing out their flaws until they feel like lepers. Martyrdom phrases, usually the mother's specialty, are often a subtler way of evoking guilt; they possess a "you owe me big time" quality that makes kids feel they need to pay for everything that has caused parental inconvenience or bother. My kids are pretty good about calling me on the carpet when I do the martyrdom thing. Lukas, my ten-year-old, usually responds with, "And we'll be right back with more of *All My Children*." Some examples of all three follow:

Guilt:

❖ "Honey, if you really loved me, you'd help me out more around the house."

❖ "You're going to be the death of me yet." (Extreme guilt!)

❖ "Can you try to get along with your brother? Every time you two fight, I get a splitting headache."

Shame:

❖ "I'm so disappointed in you for acting up in music class!"

❖ "My goodness, Tracy! You're acting like a two-year-old, throwing a fit like that!"

Martyrdom:

❖ "Okay, fine. I'll take you to school today. [Sigh] Looks like I'm the resident chauffeur around here!"

❖ "You know that if I go to your softball game, my boss will have a fit. But, I guess it's the sacrifice I have to make for being a good mom."

Phrases that provoke guilt or shame and those that turn us into a Joan of Arc encourage children to make their choices based on what will please us rather than what they think is right. You might think, "What the heck's wrong with that?" but guilt-ridden and shamed kids grow up not really knowing how to develop and follow their own internal compass. They become so accustomed to relying on us to steer their decisions that once their world extends beyond the white picket fence, they continue to seek guidance from outside influences, including nonparental ones. And as I've mentioned before, if those outside influences — such as their peers, the media, and pop-culture — don't have the children's best interests at heart as we do, or if they endorse misguided values or no values at all, they will lead children to make choices that are irresponsible, immoral, and sometimes irrevocably damaging. In addition, some of these phrases force children to bear much too heavy a burden; for example, "You're going to be the death of me yet" suggests they're respon-sible for our very survival. Sure, we're blowing smoke, but younger kids may actually believe they're pushing us one step closer to the pearly gates.

Besides, when we utter such phrases, children feel either inad-equate or compelled to protect their own sense of worth, and they will often respond with an angry counterattack or a sulky, defiant stomp off to their rooms. So, what can we do or say instead?

Instead of saying, "Honey, if you really loved me, you'd help me out more around the house,"

❖ try making an impartial observation followed by an "I" mes-sage: "You haven't helped me clean the house for several weeks. I could really use your help. It makes me feel I'm being taken advantage of when you don't help, and by the end of the day, I'm exhausted."

❖ try giving a limited choice: "When we've finished doing the housework together, then you can go to the concert with your friends."

Instead of saying, "Okay, fine. I'll take you to school today. [Sigh] Looks like I'm the resident chauffeur around here!"

❖ try making an impartial observation: "I see it's almost time for the bus to come, and you haven't eaten breakfast yet." (Throw in a casual yawn for that extra punch that says, "This is your problem, not mine. I'm sure you'll figure something out.")

❖ try using an "I" message: "I get very upset when you miss the bus day after day so that I have to take you to school."

❖ try allowing a natural consequence: "I can't be late for work anymore, so if you miss the bus, you'll have to walk, and you'll probably be late."

Instead of saying, "You know that if I go to your softball game, my boss will have a fit. But, I guess it's the sacrifice I have to make for being a good mom,"

❖ unless your job really is on the line, go to the game and enjoy it! Kids should come first whenever it's practical. But never expect brownie points or reciprocity for the sacrifices you make for them.

Instead of saying, "You're going to be the death of me yet" when the child is throwing a big tantrum in the middle of Kmart,

❖ try giving a logical consequence: "I'm going to have to take you to Aunt Laura's house so I can finish my shopping without you disturbing me or others."

❖ try providing objective information: "Other people don't like being disturbed by shouting and crying, especially when they're trying to finish their errands."

❖ try giving her a limited choice: "If you stop crying in the next two minutes, then we can stay and finish our shopping.

Otherwise, I'll have no choice but to take you home. What'll it be?" If she refuses to make the choice, say something like, "You can either choose now or I'll have to choose for you." (You and I both know what that choice will be!)

Instead of saying, "I'm so disappointed in you for acting up in music class!"

❖ try questioning: "How do you feel about your behavior in music class?" (In answering this question, the child reflects on how her behavior makes her feel about herself, which facilitates assessing herself objectively rather than relying on outside evaluation.) "How do you think your behavior affected others?" (The child answers, reflecting on the consequences her behavior has on others.) "Why do you think it's important to sit still and pay attention in class?" (When the child answers this question, she's prompted to acknowledge the presence and rationale for the rule to behave well in music class.) "What can you do to remind yourself to behave properly?" (The child answers, contemplating possible strategies to make better behavioral choices in the future.) "How do you plan on handling things to make up for your behavior?" (The child answers, reflecting on the importance of correcting her mistake by making amends.)

❖ try making an impartial observation and then providing specific information: "Ms. Dixon, the music teacher, told me you were a handful in music class today. In our family, we give our full respect and undivided attention to those who are speaking, and this includes teachers."

Instead of saying, "Can you try to get along with your brother? Every time you two fight, I get a splitting headache,"

❖ try giving a limited choice: "You two either work things out peacefully or take it outside where you can't disturb others."

❖ try the minimalist approach: Give them both a stern look, and sweep your index finger across your neck, as if to say, "Cut it out."

As you can see, these alternatives foster self-reflection, replacing attacks with guidance and a show of faith that, to a certain degree, children can handle their problems on their own. This encourages them to make responsible choices based on the values you've helped them understand and integrate rather than on someone else's opinions or values they feel obliged to adopt in order to be accepted.

Personal Insults

When we become angry or frustrated with children, it's easy to say hurtful things that attack the *child* rather than address his or her *behavior*. Whenever we attack children personally, we imply there's something inherently wrong with them. Perhaps it comes from an instinct to punish those who cause us any emotional discomfort. Perhaps we see it as a powerful tool to effect a desired change in them. But in reality, insensitive phrases simply cause injured feelings. And like us, when kids are hurt, they react with some sort of retaliatory or defensive response: shouting back, acting out, or berating themselves or us. On the rare occasion that these phrases *do* make them behave as we wish, it is *fear*, not *understanding*, that motivates them — fear of our reaction (e.g., disappointment or anger) or fear of the punishments we might cook up.

I remember my eldest daughter recounting a scene she'd witnessed between one of her best friends and the friend's father. The day before, her friend came home from high school with a B on an important algebra exam. Her father, who always demanded perfection, was furious and told her — and I quote — she was "a disgrace to the family." I've known this girl since she was in kindergarten, and she's anything but disgraceful! She's highly intelligent, very polite, and an extremely talented writer. However, she's also constantly striving for praise from others. For instance, when she was shooting hoops in our backyard and got three baskets in a row, she jumped up and down, shouting, "I did it! I'm pretty good at this, don't you think?" When she wasn't asking for compliments, she was berating herself with phrases like, "I can't do anything right," "I'm so fat and ugly," or, "Nobody likes me." Although I do all I can to undo some of the harm inflicted by her father, I'm still concerned for her self-esteem and her general outlook on life. Here are some other examples of personal insults:

❖ "You're such a bad boy."

❖ "I wish you'd never been born."

❖ "I hate you."

It's easy to see how children who assume adults are superior and therefore privy to absolute truths eventually can grow to see themselves as inadequate to the core. Even an occasional slip with one of these phrases can leave lasting scars on their self-esteem. Avoiding personal insults is therefore crucial. That said, here's an important tip to always keep in mind: the secret to resisting the urge to vent negative emotions with these phrases is to maintain calm. Here are some ways you can do just that:

❖ Always make solving their problems more important to them than to you. This way, you never take on the urgency of those problems and are thus less likely to respond emotionally with insulting phrases.

❖ Try to understand the motives behind the misbehavior rather than focusing on how it affects you. Is the rule they're breaking illogical? Does the rule no longer apply because they're getting older or circumstances have changed? Do they understand why it should be followed? Is there something bothering them that might cause them to break the rule?

❖ Try to change the way you view the child's misbehavior. Rather than perceiving it as something meant to annoy or anger you, see it as a teachable moment — an opportunity for you to help them reflect on the situation, to see to it that they experience a logical consequence, and to turn that consequence into something that will help them grow rather than tear them down.

What can we say that honors these three strategies? Let's look at some alternatives:

Instead of saying, "You're such a bad boy" when your son is whining about not getting a candy bar at the store,

❖ address what he's doing with an "I" message: "I get annoyed when someone whines to get their own way."

❖ try giving a limited choice: "You can either stop whining, or I'll have to take you home and come back without you."

Instead of saying, "I wish you'd never been born" when your older son kicks his little sister,

❖ first acknowledge his feelings: "I understand how upset you are about her scribbling on your papers,"

❖ then try questioning: "How do you think your sister felt when you kicked her like that?" (The child answers, considering the effect his actions have on others.) "How do you feel when someone hurts you?" (When the child answers, he also considers what it would be like to be in his sister's shoes.) "What would have been a better way to handle your feelings?" (The child answers, contemplating alternatives that are acceptable.) "What do you need to do to take care of her feelings?" (The child answers, acknowledging the importance of making amends to those he hurts.)

Instead of saying, "I hate you" when the child is constantly being disrespectful toward you,

❖ try providing objective information: "We use kind words, not cruel ones, in our family."

❖ try giving a limited choice that also acts as a logical consequence: "You need to leave the room. You are welcome to come back when you can talk respectfully."

❖ when she returns, get to the source of her disrespect by making an impartial observation and following up with questioning: "You seem so angry with me lately. Do you know why?" (When the child answers, she must reflect on the source of her anger. Understanding what provokes anger is the first step to expressing it constructively rather than reactively.) "How have I contributed to it?" (The child answers, while at the same time getting the message that you are willing to accept responsibility for your share of the conflict, if any. It may even encourage her to reflect on how she's contributed to it, too. What's more, by modeling accountability, you sow the seeds of this important virtue, seeds that will take root and grow over time.) "Is there anything you want me to do differently?" (This question shows her that you're willing to do what's right and reasonable to help resolve the problem, taking your demonstration of accountability one step further.

When the child answers, she also reflects on what she might do differently in this situation in the future.)

Insults can also come in the form of overheard phrases. I've heard parents make bold and disparaging statements about their children to perfect strangers as though the children were completely invisible, comments like, "These kids are driving me nuts! I can't wait to send them back to school," "He's impossible; he never sits still," or, "I don't know what's gotten into her. She's usually my good one." But believe me, kids have hearing so acute that they can give an entire cave of bats an inferiority complex. Furthermore, when we make disparaging statements about kids to others, the statements seem even more compelling than when we make them to children directly. This can cause feelings of shame, resentment, or anger — or even all three.

Other personal insults attack children's fundamental instinct to feel needed and loved by their most important pack, the family. Phrases that might make kids feel they don't belong or are not appreciated by the family include: "It was nice and quiet until you came along," "Just go away. Everyone was getting along until you opened your big mouth," and "Stop being a wet blanket. We don't need a sourpuss hanging around here." Almost all adults, and certainly those who care enough about children to read this book, don't use these phrases to intentionally threaten their children's sense of security within the family. Instead, they use them because they hope to change their behavior or vindicate themselves. Let's take a look at some alternative phrases that don't make children feel like outcasts or black sheep:

Instead of saying, "It was nice and quiet until you came along,"

❖ try the minimalist approach: Say the child's name and give the universal "hush" signal by placing your index finger to your lips.

❖ try giving a limited choice: "Either bring your voice down a notch or go outside until you do."

❖ try offering impartial feedback: "We're having trouble hearing each other over your loud voice."

Instead of saying, "Just go away. Everyone was getting along until you opened your big mouth,"

❖ try providing objective information: "Picking fights for no reason is a surefire way to disrupt the peace and ruin good moods."

❖ try giving a limited choice: "We're happy to have you join us in our card game as soon as you're willing to cooperate and behave politely."

❖ try using an "I" message: "I get irritated when someone spoils my fun by being offensive."

Instead of saying, "Stop being a wet blanket. We don't need a sourpuss hanging around here,"

❖ try offering impartial feedback that acknowledges her feelings, and ask her if she wants your help: "You seem to be pretty down in the dumps today. I make a good sounding board; do you want to talk about it?" Here, the child will either open up or refuse, dictating how you'll handle things from that point on. If the child agrees to discuss the problem and vent her feelings, let her. If she refuses, use an "I" message, then give a logical consequence: "I understand you're not willing or ready to talk about things, so until the problem is resolved or blows over, you need to go elsewhere so that you don't cast a pall on everyone in the room."

❖ try offering a limited choice: "You can stay and try to cheer up, or you can go elsewhere until you feel better."

❖ try using an "I" message: "I have faith in you to pull through this fine. If I can help, let me know. Otherwise, you'll need to go elsewhere."

In short, when children need guidance, address their behavior, not them personally. When you eliminate hurtful or degrading phrases, you can begin to see children's misbehavior as the result of choices rather than personality defects. Since choices are under their control, children can change how they choose with the help of our love, support, and guidance. On the other hand, personality flaws are neither under our control or theirs; they can't be changed by anyone. So, if we view children's actions as the result of an inherent, immutable flaw, we relinquish all power to help them make better choices in the future, and allow instead a smoldering, poisonous source of contention to eat away at our relationship with them.

Negative Rhetorical Questions

Another way we react to the annoyance or frustration we occasionally feel toward children is by posing questions to which we do not want or even expect answers. Frequently, these questions are spoken in an angry tone. Here are some examples:

❖ "Why can't you just mind me?" What's the kid going to say? "Because it's more fun minding myself."

❖ "What am I going to do with you?" I know what one of my kids would say: "Um, I dunno. Maybe send me on a Caribbean cruise with forty of my closest friends?"

❖ "What's gotten into you?" I can think of all sorts of potential replies to this one — most of them conjuring up unsavory visuals like, "I dunno...a bad case of worms, maybe?"

❖ "Do you want a spanking?" "Sure, why not? Sounds like fun!" Yeah, right!

I remember one incident in my family when my husband posed a version of this last question. We had everyone piled into the car and were headed for a nearby pizza joint when my then seven-year-old son started crying and complaining loudly. I don't even remember why. After several minutes of trying to get him to stop, my husband, who has the lowest tolerance for noise in the entire universe, couldn't take it anymore. So he shouted out an idle threat: "Do you want me to come back there and spank you?" Between sobs and hiccups and with a look of utter disbelief, Lukas replied, "Now why on earth would I want you to do that?"

When we ask rhetorical questions like these, children know we aren't the least bit interested in their answer. So, in truth, our words are just communication obstacles, not facilitators. Kids see such questions as big banners that read: "I CAN'T HANDLE YOU BY MYSELF. I HAVE NO INTEREST IN HEARING YOUR SIDE OF THE STORY, AND I ASSUME YOU HAVE NOTHING VALUABLE TO ADD." In response, children either feel so bad about themselves that they clam up or they get angry and retaliate in a verbal or physical way. Everything we say to children should have some constructive purpose — and most of what we say should be tools to guide them properly. Let's look at some alternatives:

Rather than saying, "Why can't you just mind me?" when a student misbehaves in class,

❖ try using an "I" message: "I feel angry when you refuse to follow our classroom rules."

❖ try giving a limited choice that is also a logical consequence: "You need to step outside the classroom. When you feel like you can behave, come back inside."

❖ try using the minimalist approach: say the student's name, and give him a visual cue that will remind him to behave well, like the universal index finger wag that tells him he's committing a no-no.

Instead of saying, "What's gotten into you?" when your teenager mopes around the house all day,

❖ if you don't know why she's down, try making an impartial observation, then lending a compassionate ear: "You seem to be feeling kind of low. If you want someone to listen, I'm here."

❖ if you *do* know the source of her self-pity, and it's no more justified than selling sand dunes to the Bedouins (for instance, she's upset because you didn't give in to her whining pleas for the seventy-dollar pair of shoes she saw at the mall), give her a limited choice: "Your sulking is bothering me. You need to either find a way to pull yourself out of this right now or go somewhere else until you do."

Instead of saying, "Do you want a spanking?" when your child misbehaves,

❖ try delivering a logical consequence: "You will have to leave the room until you can behave nicely."

❖ try questioning: "What is the family rule about acting up in the car?" (The child answers, prompting him to acknowledge the existence of the rule.) "Why do you think we have that rule?" (The child answers, reflecting on the rule's purpose.) "How can you express yourself and still follow that rule?" (The child answers, considering acceptable alternatives.) "How can you prevent yourself from misbehaving in the car from now on?" (The child answers, contemplating how he will correct his behavior.)

Instead of saying, "What am I going to do with you?" when a child refuses to buckle her safety belt in the day-care van after you pick her and several other kids up after school,

- ❖ try providing objective information: "It's not safe to ride in the van without seat belts fastened."

- ❖ try making an impartial observation, then giving a limited choice: "I see you don't have your seat belt on. It's dangerous to ride without fastening it. You can either buckle up right now, or I can take you off the van so you can call one of your parents to pick you up."

Each of these alternatives invites children to reflect on and take ownership of their choices. Furthermore, instead of feeling rebuffed, they feel welcomed to discuss their problem rather than defend their pride.

Positive Judgments

Even positive statements can make children feel they're being judged rather than guided, casting a dark pall of conditionality upon our acceptance of them. Such statements include positive judgments. Some address the child rather than the behavior, such as, "You're such a good boy." Others are designed to make allowances for their problems or weaknesses so they don't feel bad about themselves. For example, "Don't worry, Mikey. I had a lot of trouble spelling at your age, too." But affirmations are still subjective judgments. Some affirmations imply that our opinion of children is more accurate and reliable than their opinion of themselves. Some send kids the message that, unless they're exactly like us, we won't approve of them. This compels them to tweak their identities to our satisfaction, teaching them to make choices based on others' opinions of them, including their peers. Again, when children rely on others to evaluate them, they open their self-esteem up to attack. After all, not everyone will shower them with rave reviews. Other examples of these affirmations include the following:

❖ "What a good girl!"

❖ "It's okay, I had the same trouble asking girls out on dates."

❖ "So you didn't make the lacrosse team. I didn't play lacrosse, and I turned out okay, didn't I?" (You set yourself up for a fall with this ending.)

❖ "Honey, you're not overweight at all! You're just big boned. It runs in the family."

I'm not attempting to imply we can't comfort children, but rather than dishing out affirmations from an external source (us), we should encourage them to lick their own wounds so they don't have to look to others for comfort the rest of their lives. They need to learn to evaluate themselves in an objective manner so they can correct whatever *they* think needs changing. Here are some alternatives that do just that:

Instead of saying, "What a good girl!" when your student helps pick up the books and papers that fell out of her classmate's backpack,

❖ try providing objective information: "Helping other people makes them feel appreciated."

❖ try making an impartial observation: "I see you helped Thomas out when he spilled all his things from his backpack. He seemed so pleased that someone was willing to stop and help him instead of just rushing off to the next class."

(I'll discuss forms of praise you can use in place of these positive judgments in chapter 7.)

Instead of saying, "It's okay, I had the same trouble asking girls out on dates,"

❖ try acknowledging his feelings and offering objective information: "I understand what you're going through. I went through the same thing at your age. It's hard to stick your neck out and risk rejection, and I admire your courage in trying. If a relationship is meant to be, that girl will go out with you. If not, she'll turn you down. Everybody experiences rejection, and I don't know of a single human being that enjoys it." This differs from the original phrase because it's backed up by specific information and doesn't smack of a pardon from a higher power.

❖ try the minimalist approach: Gently pat his shoulder and say, "If you need someone to listen, I'm here."

Instead of saying, "So you didn't make the lacrosse team. I didn't play lacrosse, and I turned out okay, didn't I?"

❖ try acknowledging her feelings by offering your impartial observations: "I can see you're disappointed you didn't make the lacrosse team. I know how much you had your heart set on playing this season."

❖ try using an "I" message to point out the positive: "I really respect the dedication you showed during practices and tryouts." This statement is expressed in a way that makes it obvious that it's your opinion rather than a fact etched in stone or a verdict rendered by a judge. So, rather than swallowing the information whole and without question, the child will form her own opinion of her actions, compare it to yours, and draw an ultimate conclusion.

It's important to point out internal achievements, as in the last example. Other phrases that do this include, "I admire the courage you showed standing up for your friend," and "I respect how you honored your commitment to babysit Josh even though you were invited to your friend's party today." As a meritocratic society, we tend to focus on external achievements instead, like grades, trophies, prizes, income, and attractive physical appearance. Here are some examples of how we can emphasize virtue over more superficial, short-lived wins:

Instead of saying, "Honey, you're not overweight at all! You're just big boned. It runs in the family,"

❖ try expressing your opinion, as long as you're truthful: "Now this is only my opinion, but I think your weight is normal."

❖ voice your concerns if you think she runs the risk of developing an eating disorder: "A lot of girls become obsessed about their weight at your age. Some of them develop serious eating disorders. If you want me to take you to the doctor or a nutritionist to assess whether your weight is normal, I'd be happy to. Your concern worries me."

❖ if she is indeed overweight, offer help if she solicits it. If you, too, are carrying more pounds than you should, phrasing your statement in a way that suggests you commiserate with her may be more powerful and less likely to offend: "I think I may be putting on a few pounds, too. Maybe you and I could put our heads together and come up with an exercise program we can both enjoy. And later on, let's go to the grocery store so we can stock up on healthful foods and snacks that are low fat and low calorie. Would you like that?"

Once we remove all traces of judgment from our adult-child communication, kids no longer feel burdened by outside opinion.

When they're comfortable knowing that there's no judge scrutinizing their every thought, action, and physical imperfection, they can finally learn to assess themselves objectively. This healthy, constructive self-assessment mechanism, once fully established, frees kids from the need to rely on outside evaluations to figure out who they are and how they perform. They'll be able to use their own assessments in a way that helps them grow rather than causes them to regress. Furthermore, when making decisions, they'll choose the moral, responsible alternative because they'll be guided by benevolent selfishness rather than a fear of disapproval and rejection.

6

CONDITIONAL WORDS

*W*hen we speak to children in a way that suggests our feelings for them depend on their behavior, opinions, appearance, personality, and other aspects of their being, they try to change whatever is necessary to win our approval. But if they're busy being the kind of person *we* want them to be, how can they learn to think for themselves? How can they develop an identity according to their *own* terms? How can they design their own dreams and goals? How can they grow to rely on themselves? How can they find out what they're truly made of — the *real* them? The truth is, they can't achieve any of these things. When kids are subjected to conditional love and acceptance, their focus is on following the directions others set for them instead of charting their own course. Unfortunately, the world beyond caring adults is full of those who would lead them astray. Let's take a look at some examples of statements that imply our love and approval come with strings attached.

Qualifiers

We often add qualifiers to our expressions of both love and remorse to children. Why the addendums? They help us get our way, that's why! Placing conditions on our apologies or statements of affection sometimes gives us the leverage we need to get children to behave as we wish. As a mother of five, I can vouch for the claim that parents quickly learn what works and what doesn't; once we find a technique that gets kids to comply, we cling to it like Spandex to a wet body. Attaching strings to our approval is one of those things that consistently seems to work. But in truth, it's just our desperation talking, and what works to our immediate satisfaction sometimes causes harm down the road. Qualifiers have this effect because, in the case of expressing love, they give kids the message we'll love them, but only if they meet the criteria we set.

Since virtually everyone is externally directed to some degree, we adults want approval, too — even from children. Exposing our most intimate feelings is difficult when the possibility of rejection, however remote, looms. So, we use qualifiers when we feel too vulnerable expressing affection candidly and without stipulations. Since our own childhoods, we've learned that, next to keeping our feelings to ourselves, it's a lot easier to say, "I love you, but...," or, "I love you when...," or, "I love you if..." than to simply say, "I love you," because many of us have experienced rejection, ridicule, or criticism from people to whom we've shown affection. So, we've learned to downplay such expressions with qualifiers to lessen our chances of being hurt by those we care about. This defense mechanism often persists into adulthood, making it difficult for some to divulge unfettered affection to children. As those children grow, they often challenge our self-appointed superiority, which makes it even more difficult for us to transition from our role as disciplinarian to loving mentor.

Apology qualifiers serve a similar purpose: they're our way of justifying a wrong so we can still feel we're right. Here are some examples of both types:

❖ "I love you, but I wish you were better about cleaning your fishbowl."

❖ "I love you when you get along with your brother so well."

❖ "I'd love you if you brought Mommy a big glass of iced tea."

❖ "I'm sorry I spanked you, but you know how I hate being interrupted when I'm on the phone."

❖ "I'm sorry I raised my voice, but I'm just sick and tired of you kids shirking your responsibilities."

Can you see how, in each case, the qualifier negates the phrases it accompanies? It's as if our love or apology were never expressed, as if they've been replaced by a judgment or criticism. When children hear such qualified statements, they feel bad about themselves, angry with us, or are further driven to do whatever it takes to win our approval. Let's look at some alternatives:

Instead of saying, "I love you, but I wish you were better about cleaning your fishbowl,"

❖ try using humor: Stick a Post-it note on the fishbowl that reads, "Help! I'm smothering in my own poop! Please clean my home so I don't wind up flushed!"

❖ try making an impartial observation, then giving a limited choice: "Your fishbowl hasn't been cleaned for two weeks. If you clean it within the next ten minutes, I won't see fit to give Goldie to someone who will take better care of her."

❖ try providing objective information: "Fish need fresh, clean water to breathe."

Instead of saying, "I love you when you get along with your brother so well,"

❖ try making an impartial observation: "You and Tommy seem to have so much fun together when you two get along."

❖ try using an "I" message: "I really admire the way you interact with your little brother, even when he annoys you." (Here again, we seize the opportunity to praise internal rather than external achievement.)

Instead of saying, "I'd love you if you brought Mommy a big glass of iced tea,"

❖ try asking politely: "Laura, would you mind getting me a glass of iced tea? I'm pooped from weeding the garden out in the heat, and I'd really appreciate the favor."

Instead of saying, "I'm sorry I spanked you, but you know how I hate being interrupted when I'm on the phone," separate the apology from the discipline using any of the six types of alternative phrases. For instance:

❖ try providing objective information with your apology: "It's not polite to interrupt. Nevertheless, it is also wrong to hit. I hope you accept my apology. I should have handled things differently."

❖ try using an "I" message with your apology: "I have a hard time concentrating when I'm interrupted during a phone conversation. However, that's no excuse for my spanking you out of frustration. I should have used my words instead. I'm very sorry."

Instead of saying, "I'm sorry I raised my voice, but I'm just sick and tired of you kids shirking your responsibilities,"

❖ try providing objective information with your apology: "In our family, we take care of our responsibilities, so I expect you to take care of yours right away. Nevertheless, I had no right to yell at you. Please accept my apology."

❖ try using an "I" message with your apology: "I get frustrated reminding you to finish your chores every day. However, that doesn't make it okay for me to raise my voice at you. I should have handled things differently. I'm very sorry."

When we separate love and apologies from our discipline and expectations, we accomplish a great deal of good: First, we gain a sense of relief when we let these feelings stand by themselves. Second, we model inner strength for children when we have the courage to express intimate or vulnerable feelings; hopefully, they will grow to be comfortable expressing their own. Third, we show a certain comfort level with our shortcomings when we give children a genuine, unconditional apology, modeling for them that *being right* isn't as important as *acting right;* they then understand that it's okay to make mistakes as long as we hold ourselves accountable and try to learn from them. Fourth, in the case of phrases that address misbehavior, when we don't use qualifiers, children have no reason to retaliate in defense, so we avoid unnecessary conflict. They are therefore left to focus their attention on the behavior that needs correction as well as its consequences and solutions. Through this honest inner reflection, children can grow rather than wither with every mistake they make. Last, and perhaps most important, we show children that our love and acceptance are unconditional, that we will always love them for who they are *now* rather than who we expect them to become *later.* So, rather than spending a lifetime seeking the love and approval of others, they're free to carve out a life and an identity of their own choosing, integrating the values and principles we instill as their models and mentors.

Demanding Reciprocity

Because we have evolved into an externally directed culture, it's difficult to recognize, much less find satisfaction in, the internal rewards we reap for our good deeds. We live in a "you scratch my back and I'll scratch yours" society where all favors are expected to be reciprocated in some fashion, even if just by a show of gratitude. We're therefore programmed to seek compensation from external sources, to get something in return. Some of the words we say to children model this as well:

❖ "As long as I pay the bills around here, you'll do as I say!"

❖ "The least you could do is say "thank you" to your poor old grandpa. It took a lot of time for me to arrange this fishing trip."

❖ "Is this the thanks I get for tutoring a pack of ingrates?"

❖ "Young man, if I'm going to help you out by buying Scout Fair tickets, I expect you to repay me by shoveling the snow from my walkway."

Each of these phrases suggests children owe us. Since they imply we're dominant over children, naturally they evoke feelings of resentment and inferiority in kids. Phrases like these also suggest children don't really deserve the favors we've bestowed on them any more than they'd deserve to be knighted by the queen of England. They intimate that our good deeds are performed out of a sense of duty rather than love or compassion. The most bothersome effect these phrases have on children is that they set them up to grow into adults who sacrifice and help others only when they get something in return.

Some adults make the mistake of allowing relationships to be deeply damaged when children don't reciprocate. For instance, I know a woman who has refused to speak to her adult children for the past five years, all because they neglected to call and thank her for the Christmas cards she sent them. On the one hand, I do think it was rude for her children not to show thanks, but on the other hand, it's not her job to condemn them for their discourtesy. Their mistake is something they have to wrestle with, whether through a guilty conscience or the dictates of karma. The healthy thing for all involved would have been to communicate their differences to one another. Now, however, not only does she have no contact with them, but she has none with her six young grandchildren either. Consequently, both sides are sorely missing out on building precious memories.

I've also been guilty of expressing remarks that insist my children reciprocate for the different trials and tribulations I endure as their mother. In fact, I've done so hundreds of times in the past. The truth is, I lived in fear that if I didn't demand something in return for favors and good deeds, they'd grow up to be selfish clods. But then I realized that appreciation, generosity, and selflessness must be *inspired*, not *demanded*.

When children overhear our demands for reciprocity directed toward others, the effect can be just as harmful. Here's an example:

❖ "If the day-care director doesn't give me a promotion after all I've done to get this program accredited, I'm going to be so upset."

Here are some alternatives to the above examples that don't have the same harmful effects:

Instead of saying, "As long as I pay the bills around here, you'll do as I say!" when your child refuses to walk the dog as you've requested,

❖ try making an impartial observation and following up with questioning: "I see you haven't walked the dog yet. What's our rule about doing chores before watching TV?" (The child answers, acknowledging the rule's existence.) "Why do you think we have that rule?" (The child answers, reflecting on the reasons behind the rule.) "Good! What do you need to do now?" (The child answers, contemplating the need to change his pattern of irresponsibility and how he can correct it.)

❖ try providing objective information: "Dogs can become overweight and nervous if they don't exercise daily."

❖ try using the minimalist approach: "Brandon, the dog."

❖ try giving a limited choice: "You can either take better care of the dog or pay for someone else to do so out of your allowance."

Instead of saying, "The least you could do is say 'thank you' to your poor old grandpa. It took a lot of time for me to arrange this fishing trip,"

❖ just reap the inner rewards you get for bringing pleasure to someone you love.

❖ try using an "I" message that highlights the positives behind showing gratitude rather than the accusations of ingratitude: "I really feel good when others show appreciation for what I do for them."

❖ try modeling a phrase *they* should have made by saying, "Thank you, Grandpa," but don't insist they repeat it, otherwise they'll end up saying it out of obligation rather than sincere appreciation. This will only cause resentment. If you use this technique frequently, over time they'll internalize the gratitude you model in a form that's sincere.

Instead of saying, "Is this the thanks I get for tutoring a pack of ingrates?" when the five kids you teach after school sullenly resist doing the assignments you give them,

❖ try giving them a limited choice that acknowledges their needs: "I guess you guys need to unwind after a long day at school. What do you want to do first, eat a snack or play a short game together?"

❖ try delivering a logical consequence: "I'm going to have to reschedule tutoring to a day when you all will be more cooperative. Let's call your parents so they can pick you up early. You can take these assignments home with you and complete them before the next session." If you follow through, I seriously doubt these kids will balk like stubborn mules again.

❖ try questioning: "What's our rule about getting down to business during tutoring sessions?" (The children answer, acknowledging the existence of the rule.) "Why do you think we have that rule?" (The children answer, reflecting on the rule's rationale.) "Good! What will you do to make sure you remember this the next time?" (This question prompts the children to consider strategies that might help them make better behavioral choices in the future.) "Great idea! So, what are you going to do now?" (In response to this question, the children reflect on how they might behave henceforth and ways they can make amends.)

Instead of saying, "Young man, if I'm going to help you out by buying Scout Fair tickets, I expect you to repay me by shoveling the snow from my walkway,"

❖ be grateful to have the opportunity to help an organization's noble cause.

Instead of saying, "If the day-care director doesn't give me a promotion after all I've done to get this program accredited, I'm going to be so upset,"

❖ try to keep personal business from reaching children's ears. If you must vent to a coworker in front of your kids, say something like, "Of course, I'll be disappointed if I get passed up for that promotion, but at least I had an opportunity to help make our program one of the best in the community."

In short, when kids repay your kindness by misbehaving, they need to be disciplined. When they fail to show appreciation for your efforts, don't demand something in return; inspire gratitude by modeling it in your own behavior and by vocalizing a variety of gratitude expressions you want them to articulate in the future. Use your good deeds to model generosity and compassion, and be sure to express the satisfaction you get from giving without expecting anything in return; explain how insisting on reciprocity only cheapens that pleasure. Another way to inspire a sense of gratitude in kids is to have them write anonymous gratitude letters on a regular basis, either by themselves or with you. They can also share, either verbally or as a written list, those things and people for which they feel grateful. All these things will bring us one step closer to ridding the world of the "I'll scratch your back if you scratch mine" attitude that has become so enmeshed in our way of life.

Suggesting Unrealistic Entitlement

When we express our own sense of entitlement, the children we influence begin to believe they, too, deserve things that they should really earn instead. When we insist on rights to free parking, job security, low-cost health insurance, and so on, children absorb our every word until they, too, come to expect a free ride in many aspects of life. How is this related to external direction? Kids who feel entitled make demands on the outside world, and these demands tie them to others with a ball and chain, one so strong they become dependent on people and things in the outside world to be happy and fulfilled. If their demands are not met, they're left feeling bitter and vengeful. In other words, a sense of entitlement makes pawns of children, placing them at the mercy of external influences to satisfy their wants and needs rather than fulfilling them with their own blood, sweat, tears, and ingenuity. How many times have we let little groans of exasperation escape our lips when we hear, "But Mooommmm, what about ME!" or, "Why can't I have a big slice of pie like Adam did?" or, "I'm the oldest, so I get to sit in the front. Ha ha! So there!" These are some of children's ways of saying, "I deserve something special."

Some examples that show our own expectations for entitlement include the following:

❖ "I'm quitting that job if they start making us pay for parking!"

❖ "I can't believe Jim got a promotion and I didn't! We've both been with the company the same amount of time!"

❖ "We pay a lot of tax money to the school district. We should be able to decide what teacher Johnny will get next year!"

Each of these phrases suggests we're entitled to something to which others aren't. In reality, the only rights we truly have are spelled out in the Bill of Rights. As the following alternatives show, we must earn the rest:

Instead of saying, "I'm quitting that job if they start making us pay for parking!"

❖ try saying either nothing at all or, "Looks like the company is having cash-flow problems and may ask the employees to help pay for parking. I'm going to see if we can set up a carpool to help cut those costs. And if I can design an incentive program to boost production, I'll present it to the boss."

Instead of saying, "I can't believe Jim got a promotion and I didn't! We've both been with the company the same amount of time!"

❖ try saying nothing at all or, "I'm really happy for Jim and his promotion. Of course, I would have loved to get a promotion as well, but I'm sure that will happen eventually. I need to take a hard look at my job performance to see if there's anything I can improve. Maybe the boss can offer some constructive feedback."

Instead of saying, "We pay a lot of tax money to the school district. We should be able to decide what teacher Johnny will get next year!"

❖ try saying nothing at all or, "I sure would love to see you get Mrs. Merryman next year, because I hear she's very good with kids who need a little extra help with reading. Maybe I can write a letter to the principal pointing out why I think you two would be such a good match. If she chooses a different teacher, she may have very good reasons."

When enough children grow up understanding the importance of earning their way through life, maybe we can put an end to the entitlement that plays such a big role in the growing corruption and greed in our society. If we work to that end, we'll *truly* be entitled to the wonderful changes we help create!

7

HEALTHY *and* HARMFUL PRAISE

Since the Baby Boomers brought democracy to the family unit, raising children with high self-esteem is the brass ring: we clamber for it like a hundred head of cattle after a dwindling salt lick. (Look, you can't take the Texas out of this girl, okay?) Although pulling out all the stops to bolster self-esteem is a vast improvement over the old dictatorial upbringing most of us experienced in our own childhoods, some parents, grandparents, teachers, and other adults tend to go overboard, inflating younger children's self-worth well beyond what's real or deserved. I've seen some children get star stickers, balloons, plastic sheriff badges, and other prizes just for showing up at school for a whole week. I've seen Skittles dispensed for completing a math assignment that, after all, was the child's responsibility anyway. If I could round up all the stickers that read "Wow," "Awesome," "Great Job," and, "Way to Go!" I could paper the entire U.S. interstate highway system and still have enough left over to plaster the moon.

But doesn't it feel good to stroke the feathers of the kids we adore? You bet. And isn't it satisfying to see the sense of self-importance in their eyes and in their smiles? Sure it is. But we have to pay the fiddler eventually for our extravagance. After all, false self-esteem doesn't withstand scrutiny or attack very well; it obscures children's true identities and encourages making choices based on outside approval, which costs them dearly in the end.

Once kids wise up to what we've done, that overblown balloon explodes into a million bits. Around the time they enter middle school, they realize that, hey, they aren't the math geniuses, Olympic athletes, Pulitzer Prize–winning writers, or Nobel laureates they were led to believe they were. What's more, as soon as they're out of that "cute" stage, we adults suddenly tend to ration those positive strokes and replace them with criticisms and other negative evaluations. When children reach adolescence, many of us panic, thinking, "Oh my God. He's almost an adult, and he still has some serious kinks to work out! I have to get tough with him, or he'll wind up behind bars before he's in high school!" This drastic turnaround from being perched on a pedestal to being cast into a dark and lonely abyss can be a huge shock for kids. Sometimes the damage and confusion are so great, they take years to redress.

Some of the techniques we use to bolster children's self-esteem forestall the natural development of their inner praise mechanism, as they teach kids to define their sense of self-worth through others' eyes instead of figuring themselves out on their own. This externalized view of self encourages kids to follow outside cues to direct their behavior and choices. And with nothing productive to do, their little inner sentry falls into an ever-deepening sleep — Jiminy Cricket meets Rip Van Winkle.

However, as children's guides and mentors, we must strengthen this inner praise mechanism, not weaken it. By giving them objective feedback and encouragement rather than our opinions and evaluations, we can stimulate them to reflect on how they feel about themselves instead of what they need to do to get others to think highly of them. Let's first take a look at healthy forms of praise, and then we'll examine the harmful forms they'll replace.

Helpful Praise

Helpful praise encourages children to reflect on their own performance and abilities objectively. After repeated reflection, they develop that inner praise mechanism that can steel them against the slings and arrows of peer pressure, criticism, bullying, teasing, and other forms of judgment. Let's look at some examples:

"I" Messages

"I" messages can be used for more than discipline. They can express how a child's positive behavior makes you feel. Instead of coming off as a verdict etched in stone like some of the harmful phrases we discussed already — like "What a good girl!" — praise delivered as an "I" message is clearly presented as an opinion the child has full power to either accept or refuse. You can use "I" messages to express many positive feelings about children, but they're especially suited to praising internal achievement like integrity, compassion, and courage, as in, "I respect the way you get right to your schoolwork when you come home." Again, keep a lid on praising external achievements like getting good grades, winning sporting competitions, landing a great summer job, getting a driver's license, and so on. Although these things shouldn't go unrecognized, we need to show more appreciation when children demonstrate the fruits of their character development. Here are two more examples:

❖ "It makes me feel so good when you help me cut the grass. It's such a chore doing it by myself."

❖ "I really like the way you've been treating your little brother lately."

Impartial Observations

Our impartial observations are a way of providing children with the objective feedback they need to become aware of their actions and choices. While they shed light on misbehavior when used as a disciplinary strategy, they highlight good behavior when used as praise. For instance, consider the phrase, "You seemed to really help your friends work out their disagreement." It's completely appraisal-free; there is no message that says, "this is what you're worth" or, "keep doing whatever it is that's pleasing me if you want more of the same." So, instead of focusing on what needs to be done to remain in our good graces, children are prompted to reflect on their own performance.

Silent Praise

Think of silent praise as a spin-off of the minimalist approach we discussed in the section on discipline. So many things compete for children's attention, it's all we can do to be heard above the noise: Abercrombie & Fitch commercials, T-shirt and cap logos, Internet browsing, MP3 players, instant messaging, TV programs, movies, and on and on ad nauseum. Add our constant prattle to the mix, and it's no wonder many kids become "adult deaf." If you want to capture their attention, less is more. Just as a whisper will perk up their ears, a simple gesture will grab their interest. Both can therefore pack a powerful punch. Examples might include a nod, wink, pat on the back, smile, kiss, hug, thumbs-up, et cetera; the less said, the more genuine the message seems to be. Remember the words of William Shakespeare, "The lady doth protest too much, methinks"? When we do the yada, yada, gum-flapping thing, going on about how brilliant and good-looking and considerate and grown-up and well mannered they are, kids think, "Yeah, right. If you have to try that hard to make me feel good about myself, you're just trying to pull a fast one on me."

Overheard Praise

When a child hears praise from an adult who thinks he's out of earshot (even when that adult is *pretending* not to know he's around), the praise seems more sincere. Children don't suspect an ulterior motive; no adult is bribing, flattering, or sucking up to them in hopes they'll comply with the adult's wishes. We're talking powerful impact here, people. For instance, while you know the child is listening, but he isn't aware you know he's there, sing high praises about his accomplishment to your spouse, another family member, neighbor, a fellow teacher, friends, and others. You might say something like, "Did you see how well Anthony is playing the piano now? He's really been practicing a lot!"

Questioning

Just as in disciplining, open-ended questions prod children to reflect, to become aware of their behavior and how it affects others. In this case, however, it gets them to reflect on their good rather than bad behavior. A series of questions can guide children through a self-assessment process, while leaving our opinions, criticisms, and unsolicited suggestions out of the picture. Eventually, they'll internalize this as a self-praise mechanism. For example, if your child has just completed a big project for school, some questions you might ask are:

- ❖ "What do you think the best part of your project is?"
- ❖ "What was the most difficult part?"

❖ "What did you do to overcome that challenge?"

❖ "How did you feel when you finished the project?"

All of the above types of helpful praise are judgment-free and prompt children to think for themselves about their performance, independent of outside opinion. When they internalize this process completely, the strong inner praise mechanism that's established frees them from their reliance on outside opinion. In other words, although children can take others' opinions into consideration and perhaps even learn something valuable from them, they don't let these opinions affect their sense of worth. In short, they're in complete control of their self-esteem. Now let's look at some types of praise that don't garner such high marks.

Harmful Praise

Most people think there's no such animal as bad praise, but when praise undermines the control kids have over their own self-esteem by encouraging them to delegate that control to others, they never learn to assess themselves objectively. This is bad praise. Children who are encouraged to trust outside opinions over their own for the first several years of their lives develop the approval-seeking mentality typical of the externally directed. Usually, harmful praise involves ironclad verdicts or judgments, acceptance with strings attached, or compliments that smack of insincerity or ulterior motives. Let's look at eight categories most of us — yep, including me — have used in the past while under the delusion we were doing what was best for children.

Praising Perfection

In a society that seems to value perfection over effort, it's easy for adults to encourage flawlessness in their children. And when they come home with reams of graded papers in their backpacks, we tend to focus on the best and ignore the rest. Let's face it: I have five kids and only one refrigerator door. There are only so many "turkey hands" and "macaroni masterpieces" that can fit on my "Galerie de Fridge." And given the truckloads of schoolwork that come home every day in those five backpacks, I have to be somewhat selective. So, most of the grade-school paper trail winds up in the trash can — except those A+ geography tests and book reports plastered with "Wow, Awesome Job!" stickers. Time after time, however, I get caught red-handed. One day, my ten-year-old opened the trash can (to recover a half-eaten donut he had a change of heart over) only to discover my little "reject pile," covered in pasta sauce. The devastated expression on his face was accompanied by a howl that made me think of the albatross mating season on the Galápagos Islands: "MOOOOOMMMMMMM, why did you throw away my doggie picture? I worked so hard on it!!" Naturally, I played the part of the innocent bystander. I rushed to the trash can with a look of utter disbelief and said, "Oh my gosh! How did that get in there?" To throw him off my scent even more, I broadcast accusations throughout the house, "Oh . . . my . . . gosh . . . which one of you rascals put Lukas's doggie picture in the trash?" With no confessions forthcoming, I gently picked his artwork out of the trash, trying hard to keep pasta sauce from dripping all over the floor and hold my nose at the same time. With a reverence and tenderness that would have deeply impressed Mother Teresa, I gently wiped off as much of the pasta sauce as I could and then taped the picture up on the fridge under his skeptical but proud gaze. So what am I to do, get another refrigerator? Use all of the schoolwork as wallpaper for my den? Throw it all away?

The truth is, children need our feedback and encouragement, not our pride. If we want them to learn to assess themselves objectively rather than relying on outside opinion to do so, we must help them develop their own inner praise mechanism. For instance, in this refrigerator artwork example, you could save all the kids' work in a "gallery folder" and have rotating exhibitions where, each week, your kid chooses those pieces *he* believes deserve refrigerator door status:

❖ "What would you like to put on the refrigerator door, this colorful horse painting or this spelling test you studied so hard for?"

It's also helpful to ask children questions that help them reflect on and analyze their work:

❖ "What part of this science experiment was the hardest for you to do?"

❖ "What is your favorite part of your rainbow picture?"

❖ "Which of these do you think is your best work? Why?"

Be sure not to label any of their accomplishments as "perfect," as in phrases like, "You did a perfect job setting the table," or, "Your dragon picture looks absolutely perfect!" You don't want children to strive for perfection, because this will only make them grow to become anxious perfectionists who are perfect in only two ways: they do a perfect job annoying just about everyone else in the world and maxing out their own stress levels. Besides, I don't know about you, but I'm certainly not perfect! Our job as guides is to encourage children to strive for their personal best and to teach them that mistakes, not perfection, are what promote growth. That said, rather than use words like "perfect" or "perfection," try to say things like, "I can tell you did your personal best on this dragon picture," and "You put your all into setting the table."

Generalized Praise

Generalized praise is a form of praise that is completely devoid of specific details that one would expect in a valuable comment. Furthermore, like praising perfection, it's more about handing down a verdict than giving objective feedback. Kids subjected to generalized praise learn to rely on external rather than internal praise, and some, particularly perfectionists or those with low self-esteem, tend to automatically recall those times in the past when they didn't deserve that same praise. Such kids might even wonder if they truly deserve the praise at all. When they hear, "Wow, you did a great job cleaning your room," they might reflect back on times when their room should have been condemned by the USDA as a threat to livestock. When a teacher says, "Wow, what a great map," many kids might remember when they got a bad grade for the sloppy map they turned in the month before with all the doodling and graffiti in the margins. When some children hear, "Your hair looks wonderful today," they might think, "Yeah, right. You're my grandma. You have to say things like that to keep from having your Grandmother credentials confiscated." When some children hear, "What an awesome grade in science!" they might reflect back on the time they made a bad grade on an exam in that same course. What's more, when praise isn't substantiated with details, it comes across as empty or insincere. For instance, when we say something like, "Just look at your room! You've organized all your toys into different boxes, folded and put away all your clothes, vacuumed your carpet, made your bed, and even straightened out the video shelves," they know you really spent time analyzing their effort. However, generalized praise like, "Your room looks great," doesn't provide any details to make this comment a helpful one. Such empty phrases can lead children to believe we're being insincere — that our words are designed only to bolster their self-esteem, smooth ruffled feathers, or prepare them for some bad news. Yet they'll still use them as external beacons that show them the shortest path to winning our approval.

Confession time. I've used generalized praise as liberally as a prom queen uses mascara. But when I'd tell my teenage daughters something like, "Wow, your makeup is gorgeous," they couldn't race back to their rooms fast enough to start over. When I've said things like, "Erik, great job cleaning the dishes," he'd give me one of those "Okay, now what do you want?" looks. I guess they never trusted where I was coming from with phrases like those. Frankly, I couldn't blame them.

What can we do instead? Here are some examples that encourage children to develop inner praise:

Instead of saying, "Wow, you did a great job cleaning your room,"

❖ try using overheard praise: "Lisa spent a long time cleaning her room. I took a peek inside and, well, I have to say, an army of Mr. Cleans and Hazels couldn't have done a better job. She's made her bed, straightened out the bookshelves, organized her toys into different containers, and even alphabetized the videos. You should take a look!"

❖ try making impartial observations and providing specific information: "I see you've straightened out your room. When rooms are well organized, it's easier to find toys, clean clothing, and your other stuff. Plus, you're less likely to step on things and break them."

Instead of saying, "Wow, what a great map,"

❖ try providing impartial observations and using questioning to help the child learn to praise his own performance: "It looks like you put a lot more effort and detail into this map than you have in the past. How did you come up with that technique for shading the borders?" (The child answers, reflecting on his creative impulse.) "I see your legend contains more items, and you've labeled each landform, city, and river in different fonts and colors. How does that add to the usefulness of your map?" (The child answers, acknowledging that the detail he put into his map has turned it into a more informative one.)

❖ try using silent praise: Pat him on the back and wink as you hand him back his graded map. With one of these signals, the child might be prompted to ask himself, "What are the praiseworthy aspects of my map?" Then, he might assess those aspects one by one.

Instead of saying, "Your hair looks wonderful today,"

❖ try questioning: "How did you come up with that new hairstyle? I find it so hard to get out of my own hairstyle rut. Maybe you can help me come up with some fresh ideas."

❖ try using overheard praise: "Laura has been experimenting with new hairstyles. She seems to have a knack for knowing how to come up with different styles that match her coloring and the shape of her face. Maybe I'll ask her for some pointers."

Instead of saying, "What an awesome grade in science!"

❖ try using silent praise in the form of a nod, wink, thumbs-up, pat on the back, hug, or other nonverbal form of acknowledgment.

❖ try using an "I" message: "I really admire how hard you've been working lately in school."

Positive Labels, Comparisons, and Generalizations

Labels, comparisons, and generalizations are not always negative. We also use them as forms of praise: in fact, it's usually the most well-intentioned adult who gives children positive labels, compares them favorably to others, or generalizes their virtuous qualities. Although in our hearts we feel we're doing them a favor with these types of praise, we're really burdening them with expectations, ones they often feel unbearable pressure to live up to. These forms of praise also send children the message that we have them all figured out — they don't need to bother trying to evaluate their own performance any further because the verdict is in, and it's good. Once children see they meet with our approval, they'll stop at nothing to keep basking in our glowing admiration of them. Future choices are then determined by what will continue to make us proud of them.

With positive labels, we praise children personally, meaning we essentially pass judgment on their worth as human beings. How they feel about themselves is so crucial to their emotional well-being that many will do anything to influence that judgment in their favor. And when they learn to seek this approval at home, they'll seek it from their peers later. So it's essential to separate children's personal identities from the choices they make. As their guides and mentors, we must therefore address their behavior, not their self-worth, and nothing does a better job of this than our impartial (or objective) feedback or encouragement.

I used to say things like, "What a good girl!" or, "You're such a great kid" on a daily basis. I admit I thought I was being a great mom, but, after a while, I could see I wasn't getting the response I wanted. I thought my comments would make the needles on their self-esteem meters max out and their smiles beam, but all I really got were looks of suspicion or snide phrases like, "Gee, that's not what you said yesterday after I painted your china cabinet with black shoe polish."

Positive comparisons are simply the reverse of their negative counterparts. These phrases can put a lot of pressure on children to surpass others in every achievement and quality. Furthermore, if those with whom they're getting compared catch wind of such comparisons, it might engender resentment and, in the case of siblings, foster mean-spirited competitiveness.

Positive generalizations are also the reverse of their negative counterparts. Again, they put a lot of pressure on children to keep performing according to our highest expectations.

Of course, if someone threatened to tie my tongue to a hot tailpipe and drag me naked over broken glass if I didn't make a choice between the negative and positive versions of these three types of judgments, I'd take the latter hands down. I hear all sorts of adults whom I consider good people — including other parents, teachers, grandparents, school counselors, and even police officers — lavish children with, "You're such a strong boy," "You're always so respectful toward your elders," or, "You're one of the brightest kids in my class." These folks care deeply about kids, and they'd be truly horrified if they understood the full effect of such phrases. Let's look at some examples of each along with alternatives that can spare them the wrong message:

Instead of saying, "You're such a good girl,"

❖ try using an "I" message: "I really respect the compassion you showed when you comforted that little boy after he was teased." Again, notice how internal rather than external achievement is praised.

❖ you can also follow up with questioning to help her generate the internal dialogue necessary to develop inner praise: "How do you think he felt when you helped him like that?" (The child answers, contemplating the effects of her kindness on another.) "How did it make you feel?" (The child answers, reflecting on how showing compassion affects her.) "What kind of impact do you think you made?" (The child answers, thinking about how her actions might have made a difference in someone else's life.)

Instead of saying, "You're such a smart boy,"

❖ try making an impartial observation: "You're doing very well in my class. You must really enjoy working hard and learning new things."

❖ try using overheard praise by discussing his talents with a fellow teacher: "It's amazing how quickly James learned to make spreadsheets in my computer class. I might have to get him to teach some of his classmates a thing or two."

Instead of saying, "You look so pretty today!"

❖ try making an impartial observation: "You put a lot of effort into looking nice for your date with Billy. That shows such consideration for him."

❖ try using an "I" message: "I really admire how well you co-ordinate your clothes and come up with so many creative hairstyles."

Instead of saying, "You're the brains of the family,"

❖ try using an "I" message: "I admire how dedicated you are to your schoolwork."

❖ try using overheard praise: "That Tommy can figure out assembly directions on just about anything! He doesn't even need to read the manual half the time."

Instead of fostering an unhealthy sense of competition with phrases like, "Who's the best little boy in the whole wide world?"

❖ try telling the child you love him, sharing some of the little things that make him special to you.

❖ try using silent praise, like a big bear hug. (But beware: the praise will no longer be silent if you squeeze too hard and the child starts to scream or moan.)

Instead of saying, "You always start your homework right when you come home from school!"

❖ try making an impartial observation that also describes the benefits of the child's good choice: "You finished your homework right away instead of putting it off. Looks like you've allowed yourself two extra hours to play!" (Notice how the second part of this phrase implies the child is the master of his own destiny, unlike, "You finished your homework right away. For that, I'll allow you to have two extra hours to play!")

❖ try silent praise: When the child finishes his work, give him the thumbs-up or a pat on the shoulder.

Instead of saying, "You never forget to thank Aunt Sally for her birthday gifts,"

❖ try making an impartial observation: "I notice that, just like last year, you thanked Aunt Sally for the gift without me having to remind you."

❖ try questioning: "How do you think it makes Aunt Sally feel that you remember to thank her for the birthday gift she sends you?" (The child answers, reflecting on the effect his actions have on others.) "How does it make you feel to be so responsible like that?" (When the child answers this question, he also considers how being considerate of others benefits him.)

Instead of saying, "You never make bad grades!"

❖ try using overheard praise: "I can't remember a time when Bobby had trouble with his schoolwork. He must really enjoy learning."

❖ try using an "I" message: "I really respect the effort you put into your academics."

Instead of saying, "You're the fastest kid in the school!"

❖ try making an impartial observation: "You've been training faithfully for the past two months, and all your hard work has paid off: you've run your best and come in first."

❖ try making an impartial observation combined with questioning: "You've won the last five races! Why do you think you were able to accomplish that?" (The child answers, reflecting on how his hard work paid off so that he was able to meet his goal of winning.)

Praising the Rewards
Rather Than the Journey to Success

Because we live in a culture that is so meritocratic, it's easy to focus on trophies, ribbons, awards, grades, and other representations of achievement rather than the effort involved in attaining them. Just the other day, I overheard one of my friends, someone I consider to be a wonderful parent, say to her nine-year-old son: "Don't you want to join the swim team this year? I mean, you get all sorts of cool trophies and ribbons!" There was no mention of the benefits he'd reap other than material accolades — no discussion of the physical fitness gains, the new friendships that could be formed, the new swimming skills he could acquire, the inner strength he could get learning to rebound from defeat, or the social skills he could gain working together with other team members.

When children let these external symbols overshadow the internal struggle they go through to achieve a particular goal, they have one more motive to steer their choices with external beacons, choices made to gain outside approval. I can't think of a more tangible way for a child to beg for pack acceptance than a child parading around an Olympic-size swimming pool with a shiny trophy raised above his head. Competitions in which emphasis is placed on getting the prize create a deep division between those with trophies and those without, winners and losers.

Children don't need the world to categorize them according to how full their trophy cabinets are. They need to be able to evaluate how hard they tried, how much they learned, how well they handled failure, and how long they persevered to reach their goal. Let's look at some examples of praise that emphasize the goals, as well as the healthier alternatives that focus on the journey kids must take to reach those goals:

Instead of saying, "Wow, you made all A's,"

❖ try using an "I" message: "I really admire how enthusiastic you are about learning."

❖ try making an impartial observation: "You seem to have a really good understanding of math and science."

Instead of saying, "First place trophy! Great job!"

❖ try using overheard praise: "Johnny really worked well with his team to come from behind in the last inning."

❖ try using silent praise: A nod, thumbs-up, or wink should do.

Instead of saying, "Good going — a second-place trophy for the soccer match!"

❖ try making an impartial observation: "You seemed to encourage your teammates so well when they were behind three goals to one."

❖ try questioning: "Did you notice how well your teammates played together?" "Did you notice how much your kicks have improved since the last game?" "Did you have fun?" These questions encourage the child to consider benefits of the soccer match aside from winning the trophy.

Excessive, Indiscriminate, and Insincere Praise

Excessive, indiscriminate praise makes it difficult for children to judge themselves realistically. Consider the unfortunate kid whose grandma praises him so incessantly, that by the sound of her motor mouth, you'd think she was the Energizer Bunny on a sugar high: "Oh that Tommy isn't he the sweetest little boy why he's as cute as a bug I bet he makes straight A's in school don't you dear never mind I know you do (inhale) and he's the quarterback on the middle school team should've been first string but those dopes don't know how talented that boy is and would you look how gorgeous that hair is (inhale) reminds me of Antonio Banderas on a good hair day and those eyes could charm the scales off a snake . . . [blah blah blah blah]."

As with generalized praise, this kind of praise can backfire, because when kids venture into the real world, if they are mediocre, at best, at whatever they were told they excelled at, or the talents they were led to believe they were born with turn out not to exist, they might feel it was nothing but a cruel con game. In fact, this false perception of greatness may even have kept them from bettering themselves in those areas in the first place. After all, when you're nearly perfect, why should you bother? But when they finally reach the realization that they're not as wonderful at everything as the adults in their lives promised, the opposite effect occurs — their self-esteem crumbles like a ten-day-old cookie.

Overly gushy praise usually doesn't sit well with children of any age. In fact, it often annoys them, because they think they're being treated like babies. You've seen the looks on children when an adult pinches their cheeks with fingers that could be vise clamps, talking in a high-pitched voice that would make anyone's stomach turn: "How's my precious little Pooh Bear? Just as gorgeous as his daddy. You're going to break those hearts, aren't you, Sweetie Weetie? Koochy, koochy, koo." The poor kid's rolling his eyes, trying to smile politely. But privately he's fretting over when the bruises will fade and the blood will return to his cheeks. To most kids, this overly unctuous gushing comes off as a bit insincere. Plus, this type of praise does nothing to stimulate the internal dialogue children need to assess the true nature of their talents, behavior, and skills. They're too engrossed in thinking, "Yoo hoo? I'm not in diapers anymore. You can stop treating me like a little baby!" Any of the five helpful praising styles we've used are alternatives that can inspire internal rather than external direction.

The Most Common Offender: "I'm So Proud of You!"

I know I, for one, have uttered those five little words a jillion times, all the while thinking I was such a good mommy to do so. But now I realize that, with this phrase, I was fostering external direction. Why? Because it tells them: "Let my level of pride be how you measure your performance and self-worth so you can base your future decisions on how proud they're going to make me."

It's important to repeat: children truly don't need our pride. The centuries-old myth that they must have our approval to learn how to think and act responsibly has contributed to our detour to external direction. Look around at the mess our world is in now. What better proof do we need that just because we've encouraged children to make adults proud generation after generation doesn't make it a beneficial practice?

What children *do* need is our support, guidance, impartial feedback, and encouragement. These things are altogether different from expressing pride, in that we do not assume the role of judge and jury. Instead, we remain children's wise and benevolent mentors who will love them unconditionally for who they are now, rather than love them conditionally for who we expect them to become later.

So, what can we say instead? After all, there are many times when we do feel proud of the children we love. Will we be drawn and quartered for expressing that pride? Do we have to slink furtively into dark alleys to sing our praises? Thankfully, we don't have to resort to these extremes. There are ways to express feelings of pride without encouraging approval seeking and external direction. For instance, you can say things that evoke introspection and inner praise like, "I bet you're proud of yourself!" or, "You must be proud." When children hear these phrases, they're likely to think things like, "Hmm, am I proud? Well, yeah, I guess I am. After all, I worked extra hard on this assignment." Furthermore, we can vent our pride through many of the healthier forms of praise already discussed, particularly "I" messages like, "I really admire how hard you've been working on your schoolwork."

In short, praise should not be a verdict rendered by judge or jury. It should be fair, sincere, and realistic feedback for children's accomplishments, and it should encourage them to develop the inner praise mechanism that allows them to rely on objective self-assessment instead of outside opinion. No one is better equipped to evaluate their performance and character than the children themselves, because they alone possess the keenest awareness of their own goals, priorities, strengths, weaknesses, and experience level.

8

WORDS THAT TELL KIDS ADULTS ARE SUPERIOR THINKERS

*b*ecause we're older, wiser, and more experienced than children, it's only natural for us to assume we know better than them. And we usually do, especially when they're young. (Of course, from their perspective, our IQs plummet at least thirty points when they become teenagers.) But when we capitalize on this assumption of superiority by telling them what opinions they should have, belittling or criticizing their ideas, pressuring them to conform to society's standards, and using phrases that are vestiges of the authoritarian family era like "I told you so," or "Because I'm the boss, that's why," we instill a sense of inferiority, helplessness, resentment, indignation, or any combination of these. Furthermore, such phrases promote external direction in the following ways:

❖ Children think adults will always know better than they do about everything. Their whole mind-set becomes "I don't know how to think very well. Since I can't come up with my own ideas and opinions, I need to rely on adults to do that for me." Later on, they transfer this attitude to peers they consider more powerful, more experienced, or just plain tougher, especially when they enter that phase of seeing us as dumber than a sack of hammers.

❖ Since we know so much more, children assume that we are superior as beings overall. This superior/inferior relationship makes them fight even harder for our approval when they're younger. That approval-seeking mentality becomes so deeply ingrained it's hard for them to shake it. As adolescents, and then as adults, they seek peer approval.

❖ When we tell children what to think all the time, there's little reason or opportunity for them to practice thinking on their own. The internal dialogue so crucial to considering pros, cons, consequences, and alternatives never fully develops. In other words, they grow up with very poor introspection skills.

❖ When adults are always hovering over kids, telling them what they should think, what opinions they should have, and how little they really know, those kids who don't fall for it hook, line, and sinker get angry and annoyed. Wouldn't you? We've all been cornered by know-it-all adults at the company Christmas party, a family reunion, or some other event where a quick escape is hard to come by. Listening to a didactic tirade that goes on and on like a broken record is nothing short of absolute torture for two reasons: it's boring and it's insulting. What such braggarts are really telling us is this: "What I'm saying is right. Don't even bother challenging me because you are W-R-O-N-G." Get trapped by someone like this and you may as well hand the guy a sledgehammer, slip into an iron maiden, and tell him to swing away.

Kids have limits on what they can tolerate, too. In fact, it's actually healthier for kids to get upset with know-it-alls than to believe everything they hear without question. However, this is often not an indication that they have enough confidence in their own thoughts to take offense when someone else doubts or disputes them. Their feathers are usually ruffled because their pride, and therefore their self-esteem, has been attacked. So they defend themselves with barbed words or behavior that is sullen or angry. What's worse, when in the midst of a counterattack, kids are not engaged in rational introspection.

I saw a *Family Circus* comic strip recently that says it all: a little girl, looking up at her mother with a reverent expression, asks, "Do I have any strong opinions?"

We tell children what to think in a variety of ways. Some are blatantly hostile, while others are deceptively benign. Let's take a look at five broad categories.

Thought Indoctrination

Whereas criticism, judgments, and harmful praise have an indirect way of shaping children's beliefs, thought indoctrination does so more directly. Thought indoctrination phrases are those which tell children what they *should* be thinking. In fact, many of them begin with "you should," "you ought to," or "you must." Take a look at these examples. They should demonstrate what constitutes thought indoctrination, as well as reveal how extensively these phrases pervade our adult-child communication.

❖ "You should be proud of yourself for making the debate team." With this phrase, the student is being told how he *should feel* about an accomplishment. If it's no big deal to him, he might wonder if it should be. Or he may think that since it's important to you, he better keep living up to your expectations lest he fall from grace.

❖ "You should be ashamed, hitting your little brother like that. He's only four!" This example is both a shaming and a thought indoctrination phrase. Again, the child is being told how to feel about herself. Furthermore, she hasn't had a chance to share her side of the story, and her feelings have not been acknowledged. Does that mean she can't feel angry as well — or sorry? Or compassionate?

The next three examples have similar effects:

❖ "You must feel embarrassed about saying those bad words in class. It's disgraceful."

❖ "You ought to be very angry with Tom for spreading those rumors about you."

❖ "Don't be ridiculous! You don't hate your sister."

As you can see, they all suggest children are either not thinking or feeling when they should, or their thoughts or feelings are flawed. Now let's see how we can replace these with healthier alternatives:

Instead of saying, "You should be proud of yourself for making the debate team,"

❖ try making an impartial observation: "I see all your debate practice has paid off. It must feel great to see your efforts rewarded." You can also point out the ways in which this achievement may benefit her long-term goals: "Since you want to be a lawyer, these skills may prove valuable in your career."

❖ try using questioning: "How do you feel now that all your hard work has paid off?" (The child answers, contemplating the benefits of her long hours of practice.) "What other areas of your life do you think your debating skills will improve?"

(Again, when the child answers this question, she must think about how her debating skills can carry over into social settings, like interpersonal conflict resolution, and career settings, like negotiations, among other things.)

❖ try using overheard praise: Tell another adult how hard she practiced and what a skilled debator she's become as a result.

Instead of saying, "You should be ashamed, hitting your little brother like that. He's only four!"

❖ try providing objective information: "We use words, not hitting, in our family."

❖ try delivering a logical consequence: "Since you're too angry to deal with your problem with Jimmy, you need to sit here with me until you cool off and until I'm sure you won't hurt him or anyone else. We'll talk about it once you calm down."

❖ try giving a limited choice: "You can either play nicely with your brother, or you can go upstairs and play alone."

Instead of saying, "You must feel embarrassed about saying those bad words in class. It's disgraceful,"

❖ try providing objective information: "Even though they may laugh, kids usually feel embarrassed and uncomfortable when they hear bad words."

❖ try delivering a logical consequence: "You'll need to go to the principal's office so that I know you won't be using that kind of language in front of the other students again."

❖ try using the minimalist approach: Say the child's name in a stern voice and give him that evil eye that parents, grandparents, and teachers have honed to perfection over the centuries.

Instead of saying, "You ought to be very angry with Tom for spreading those rumors about you,"

❖ try using questioning: "How did you feel when you found out what Tom had done?" (The child answers, reflecting on how Tom's behavior made him feel.) "Why do you think he spread those rumors?" (The child answers, reflecting on the motivation some people have to gossip about others.) "How do you plan to handle it?" (To answer this question, the child must ponder different options to solving his problem.) "I had something like that happen to me when I was around your age. Do you need any help or suggestions from me?" (The child answers, feeling acknowledged and comfortable in knowing that you can relate to him and he can turn to you for help if necessary.)

❖ try making an impartial observation: "You seem very mad about what happened between you and Tom today." This might help open up dialogue between you and the child. Rather than give unsolicited advice, wait to see how he responds.

❖ try providing objective information: "It's upsetting when a friend spreads bad rumors behind another friend's back. It makes it difficult to decide whether that friendship should be salvaged and if so, how to go about it."

Instead of saying, "Don't be ridiculous! You don't hate your sister,"

❖ try using an "I" message followed by an open-ended question that prompts reflection about how such behavior would affect him if the tables were turned — in other words, a question that encourages empathy: "I feel hurt when someone I love says they hate another person I care about. How do you think you would feel if someone you looked up to treated you that way?"

❖ try making an impartial observation and then using questioning that explores what triggered the conflict: "You two seemed to get along so well this morning. What's different now?" (The child answers, reflecting on those factors or events that led to the disagreement.)

❖ try using questioning that encourages further introspection: "Why are you upset with your sister?" (The child answers, exploring the root of his anger.) "What are more acceptable ways of letting her know how you feel?" (The child answers, considering how he could have expressed his anger constructively.) "What do you need to do to solve this problem?" (The child answers, pondering ways to make amends with his sister.)

Each of these alternatives gives children the opportunity and the self-confidence to think their own thoughts, generate their own opinions, and come up with their own solutions. Another plus: most of them help open up dialogue. What better opportunity to give them the guidance and mentoring they need to resolve a problem?

Invalidators

Sometimes we dismiss children's opinions by using invalidators, phrases that tell them their thoughts and opinions are incorrect or unjustified. And even those meant to mend hurt feelings or bolster self-worth can promote external direction by suggesting children don't know how to think or form opinions properly. Here are some examples of various types of invalidators — punitive and comforting:

❖ "You don't understand! If you wake up late every morning, I risk being late for work myself!" Any phrase prefaced by "you don't understand" tells children their minds are incapable of grasping even the most rudimentary concept. But how do we know they don't understand?

❖ "You're wrong. Your teacher isn't mean at all." When it comes to things that are impossible to prove, no one has special access to the absolute truth. To tell children they're wrong because you disagree with them can incite ire in the smallest of them. It's better to say something like, "I disagree" instead.

❖ "No you don't look fat! Stop talking like that!" Although phrases like this one are designed to make children feel better about themselves, they nonetheless suggest we know better than they do and that they therefore need to rely on our opinions about them rather than their own. When kids ask adults about their appearance, they're often looking for strokes of flattery or reassurance. However, as we will soon see, telling them their thinking is wrong is not the best approach.

❖ "No, Austin is not warmer than Houston in the summer." Even though we may be right about what we view as objective facts, whenever we invalidate what kids say, their developing brains never grow a leg to stand on. What confidence they have in their own thinking is shaken.

I recently heard a father, out shopping with his five- or six-year-old son, gently utter invalidator after invalidator like, "No, you don't like that brand of cereal. It tastes bad. You really don't want it." By refuting his son's opinions and stating his own as though they were absolutes, he's fostering external direction in that child — it makes no difference that he said them in a kind voice. Children who are invalidated by adults day after day don't have much confidence in their own ability to form reliable opinions. In fact, they eventually believe that kids don't have the same rights to an opinion as adults do. Let's see how we can reword these examples in a way that encourages internal rather than external direction:

Instead of saying, "You don't understand! If you wake up late every morning, I risk being late for work myself!"

❖ try using an "I" message: "I really get upset when I'm late for work because you get up too late to catch the bus."

❖ try delivering a logical consequence: "I can't afford to be late to work anymore. If you miss the bus again, I'm afraid you'll have to walk or bike to school."

❖ try using questioning: "How do you think I feel when I'm late for work because I have to drive you to school when you miss the bus?" (The child answers, reflecting on the consequences her tardiness has on others.) "How would you feel if I were to pick you up late after school?" (The child answers, contemplating how a similar situation would affect her if the tables were turned. This introspection helps her develop empathy skills.) "What do you need to do to make sure you wake up in time to catch the school bus every morning?" (To answer this question, the child must think of strategies to help her get ready for school on time.) "What would you do if you were in my shoes?" (The child answers, pondering potential consequences that might be levied.)

Instead of saying, "You're wrong. Your teacher isn't mean at all,"

❖ make it clear that you're stating an opinion, not a fact blessed by a higher being. You can do this by using an "I" message: "I've always had nothing but pleasant experiences with her. Unless I'm not seeing another side of her, she seems nice enough to me."

❖ try questioning: "What is it about her that you don't like?" (When he hears this question, he feels acknowledged rather than criticized for his opinion. To answer, he must explore the root of his ill feelings.) "What has she done that you think is mean?" (When the child answers this question, he must come up with reasons that make sense. If there are none, this question might encourage him to come to grips with any inner dishonesty clouding his judgment.) However, it's not always necessary to delve deeply into things like this, because sometimes children just want to vent their feelings without being pelted by advice or offers to help.

Instead of saying, "No you don't look fat! Stop talking like that!"

❖ try making an impartial observation along with offering some open-ended questioning: "It seems like a lot of girls your age are concerned about their weight, even when their weight is healthy. Have you noticed that, too?" (The child answers, reflecting on the overly low weight standards set by peers and popular culture and whether or not she has fallen prey to those distorted standards.) "What do you think is causing this perception?" (The child answers, reflecting on the basis of those unhealthy standards.) "Do you know anyone who is so concerned with her weight she's too thin or even looks ill?" (The child answers, pondering various friends or acquaintances misled by such standards and how their lives may have been affected.)

❖ try using an "I" message: "I get worried when you say you're overweight. I don't want you to get so thin that you become sick."

❖ try providing objective information: "According to the Metropolitan Weight and Height Standards, weighing one-hundred-one pounds is considered well within normal range for a girl five feet, two inches tall."

Instead of saying, "No, Austin is not warmer than Houston in the summer,"

❖ try using an "I" message. "I may be wrong, but I thought the hill country was less humid than the coastal region. That would make Austin cooler in the summer. We can find out more about it together, though. Let's see what our encyclopedia says."

❖ try making an impartial observation and then using questioning: "If the coast is near water, it seems like it would be more humid. Would that make it hotter or cooler than drier places?" (The child answers in a manner appropriate to his grade and knowledge base.) "Let's look it up just for fun. We might both learn something!"

❖ try providing objective information: "Austin is at a higher altitude than Houston. It's also drier."

Instead of saying, "No, you don't like that brand of cereal. It tastes bad. You really don't want it,"

❖ try using an "I" message to express your own opinion and take the opportunity to show that differences in opinions and tastes are acceptable: "That cereal is a little bit too sweet for me. I'm glad we have differences in opinions sometimes. If people all liked the same things, it'd be a pretty boring world."

❖ try using an "I" message and then providing objective information: "I don't care for that kind of cereal. But everyone has a right to their opinion."

❖ try giving a limited choice: "Okay, why don't you pick out one cereal that's your favorite, and I'll pick out a few that most everyone else in the family will enjoy." (Or we can use an example that's more clearly a choice: "What would you like as your cereal choice, Honeycombs or Cap'n Crunch?")

It's also very powerful to ask children's opinions. Most kids are so unaccustomed to adults giving a hoot about what they think, they're absolutely flabbergasted when we ask things like, "So, what do you think I should plant in my new flower bed?" or, "Do you think the Cowboys will win this year?" or, "Can you help me decide how to decorate the classroom for the Valentine's Day party? You have such good ideas for decorating things." This nurtures their sense of self-respect, encourages them to form their own ideas, and builds confidence in their ability to create their own opinions in the first place. Even if you disagree with their responses, remember to accept their opinion for what it is — their opinion. Don't refute, criticize, or ridicule something they have every right to express.

When we communicate in ways that get children to think rather than cause them to doubt their own ideas and opinions, not only will we go far in preserving harmony within our relationship with children, but they will learn to develop and make sense of their own values, beliefs, and identity. This is a crucial element in guiding children to become self-directed adults with rock-solid self-esteem.

Pressuring Children to Conform

Because of our own desire for acceptance, many of us aren't comfortable around children who stick out like sore thumbs. First of all, if we're their parents, grandparents, or other guardians responsible for the way they dress and act, we live in fear that they're going to make us look bad. I remember when my seven-year-old daughter went through a phase during which she would clasp locks of her hair with Chip Clips (the plastic clips designed for closing bags of potato chips) in an assortment of sizes and colors so that each one of her tresses was pointing in a different direction. Not only did every bag of chips in the house go stale within a couple of days, but I swear she looked like a mutant version of Pippi Longstocking. Scary. I would cringe every time she left for school because I just knew the teachers and other parents would think I either was negligent, had passed along a defective fashion gene, or was completely off my rocker. But then I decided this was *her* hair and *her* preferences, not mine. If I insisted she conform to current hairstyles, she would only feel angry with me, bad about her looks, and hesitant to express her creativity in a way that might not meet with others' approval. I felt my resolve waver a bit when she left for school wearing a yellow plaid shirt and a purple paisley skirt, but then, that's a chapter unto itself.

Another reason we pressure kids to conform is that nonconformity scares us. When they express their own individuality and march to the beat of a different drum, we begin to worry, "What's wrong with this kid?" In truth, there's nothing wrong with children being bold enough to express themselves. We adults could learn from their free-spiritedness. I'm not yet up to decorating my hair with Chip Clips, but thanks to my daughter's ever-changing, unique fashions, I'm trying to spread my own wings in that area. When you think about it, there's something wrong with a society that won't accommodate the freedom to express oneself. Here are some examples of how we pressure kids to conform:

❖ "You aren't wearing your hair like that, are you?"

❖ "You can't wear a blue shirt with those black slacks. Go upstairs and change, now."

❖ "You still like the Backstreet Boys? Aren't they a little passé now?"

❖ "You can't wear army boots with shorts! You'll be a laughing-stock!"

❖ "You're not supposed to color horses blue. There's no such thing." (So much for that kid's blue period.)

The only real alternative to these statements is silence. Let children develop their own tastes and style. Let them explore different ways of expressing themselves. More often than not, they'll pull to center, but if they don't, so what? Take a look at Albert Einstein and Georgia O'Keeffe: both were considered oddballs but would make great role models for anyone — child or adult.

"Children Are to Be Seen and Not Heard"

Phrases of the "seen, not heard" variety date back to those prehistoric times of our own childhoods. Typical of the authoritarian style of parenting, adults viewed children in an almost dehumanized way. Children were often allowed fewer basic rights than adults, including the right to voice an opinion, belief, idea, or other thought. Of course, most of us don't look upon children this way now. Some of my children express themselves so much it's all anyone else can do to get a word in edgewise. But even though many of us promised ourselves as children we'd never repeat such phrases to our kids, sometimes it's hard to resist. After all, they're so deeply ingrained, most likely from our own parents, particularly our fathers, that it's easy, almost automatic, to say them when the chatter reaches the fingernails-on-the-chalkboard level.

Examples of phrases that belong to this category would include, "Shut up and listen," "Just hush, and do as you're told," "I don't want to hear a peep out of you," "Stay out of my way," "Listen and learn," and "If I wanted your opinion, I would have asked for it." Each of these and phrases similar to them can have many possible negative effects on children. In kids who know perfectly well they aren't inherently inferior to adults — that they're just smaller, younger, and less experienced — such words breed resentment. They might respond by sulking, getting angry, or thinking pretty ugly thoughts about us. In any case, the harmony in our relationship with kids takes a giant step backward. Those who actually *do* consider themselves inferior to adults suffer the biggest blow: damage to their self-esteem. This widens their perceived kid/grown-up "value gap" even more, until they start seeing themselves as substandard thinkers. As soon as this happens, such kids come to entrust many of their decisions, beliefs, and opinions to adults, and later, of course, to their peers, the media, and popular culture. They might also feel resentful toward us, but that resentment is usually a product of their injured pride rather than a sense of injustice or inequality. In all of these scenarios, children don't have the presence of mind to think clearly about whether or not the phrases they've heard were justified, and whether or not they do have something valuable to contribute.

What can we say instead of these and similar phrases? When children are simply discussing one of their ideas or opinions, we should show the same respect we'd expect others to show us: listening attentively and avoiding invalidators. After all, everyone has the right to express themselves — and this certainly includes children. But if they're overstepping the reasonable bounds of polite conversation by yammering on when others are trying to talk too or when it's not the right time or place for you to listen (for me, this usually happens when I'm behind any locked bathroom door), there are alternative phrases you could use instead. Here are some examples:

❖ Try giving a limited choice: "If you're quiet for just a moment, I'll be able to finish what I'm doing and pay better attention to what you're saying."

❖ Try providing objective information: "It's impolite to talk when someone isn't in a position to listen," or, "In our school, we wait to talk until we're sure the other person is able to listen."

❖ Try using questioning: "What's our rule about talking to others when they're too busy to listen?" (The student answers, acknowledging the existence of the rule.) "Why do we have that rule?" (The student answers, reflecting on the consequences his behavior has on others.) "What do you need to do now?" (The student answers, contemplating ways to make it up to the class and strategies for recognizing cues that might signal whether a person is ready to listen, while using self-restraint until they are.)

❖ Try using the minimalist approach: Say the student's name and place your index finger to your lips.

Listening to children can be tiresome, particularly when they're young. It takes a lot of patience to wait for them to finish their thirty-minute spiel on how Mary Caroline put chewing gum in Emma's long black hair. But, think hard before shooing them away. When, in order to give children your undivided attention, you push away from the keyboard, take a break from the housework, or put that book aside (yes, even this one), you send them a powerful message: you have faith in them to think on their own, you consider them important enough to place your own agenda on hold, you acknowledge they might have something interesting to say, and you are just as willing to learn from them as they are from you. Wow!

"I Told You So" Phrases

I can't begin to count the number of times the four little words "I told you so" have spewed out reflexively from my mouth. The same holds true for their cousins: "You had that coming," "That'll teach you," and "I knew this would happen." Every time I uttered one of these phrases, it was as though I were saying, "Silly you! You can't possibly come up with good choices on your own! That's what I'm here for. Let me decide for you, so you won't mess up." I knew full well, however, that I wouldn't consider for a moment saying the same thing to another adult. If I told my best friend, "I told you so," or, "I knew this was going to happen," when she messed up, I might as well add that irritating, singsong chant every kid says when someone gets in trouble: *"Nah-nah-nah-nah-nah."* She'd probably give me the silent treatment for months, and frankly, I wouldn't blame her.

When we say these kinds of phrases to kids, they might react with something like, "Man, she thinks she's such a know-it-all. She must think I'm still teething, for God's sake. Everyone makes mistakes. Why can't she just leave me alone?" Some might express this out loud. Some might keep it to themselves until the resentment builds to a boiling point and they blow their tops. Others might respond physically by either hitting an unsuspecting sibling unlucky enough to be within reach, slamming a door so hard the plaster shatters from the ceiling, or punching some inanimate object that can't hit back.

The worst reaction, though, is when children turn against themselves. For instance, if a child hears, "I told you softball was the wrong choice for you! Most of the kids in our neighborhood league are a year older than you and have attended softball training camp every summer for several years," he might beat himself up with thoughts like, "I knew I should have listened. Who am I kidding, trying out for the softball team. Dad told me the competition was tough this year. I'm such a loser." Not exactly the yellow brick road to self-esteem.

Whether their reaction is inward or outward, kids won't be

thinking about the choice they've just made, its consequences, how to avoid making the same mistake in the future, and how to solve the problem created in its wake. Instead, they'll be ruminating over how coldhearted we are or what idiots they are. Besides, who likes to have their nose rubbed in their own mistakes? It just puts up one more roadblock to learning how to rebound from failure, one more thing fostering external over internal direction.

They hear this message enough, and it's no wonder children begin to doubt themselves. They look expectantly to our facial expressions, comments, or guidance in response to everything, from what shirt to wear with those khaki pants to whether they should invite Katie or Kellie to spend the night Saturday. We, and later their peers, the media, and popular culture, become the external beacons steering them through life. Here are some examples and alternatives. Some of these comments anticipate the child's mistake while others follow it:

Instead of saying, "Didn't I tell you not to run on the dock?" after the child falls,

❖ try providing objective information: "It's not safe to run on the dock."

❖ in light of the natural consequence of falling, try giving an "I" message: Say with as much empathy as you can muster, "I'm sorry you forgot about our rule not to run on the dock. I can see that fall hurt, and I'm sorry you scraped your knee, but running in those shoes on a slippery dock is usually going to result in a fall just like that one."

❖ try using questioning: "What's the rule about running on the dock?" (The child answers, acknowledging that the rule exists.) "Why do we have that rule?" (The child answers, reflecting on the rationale behind the rule.) "What can you do to remember that rule next time?" (To answer this question, the child must come up with strategies that will help him remember to walk on the dock in the future.)

Instead of saying, "I told you not to wait too late to start your homework" when your child complains that he's too tired to do it,

❖ try making an impartial observation before it gets to that point: "I see it's nearly dinnertime and you haven't started your homework yet."

❖ try delivering a natural consequence: If he doesn't finish his homework in time, he'll have to deal with his teacher's reaction. Simply say something like, "That's between you and Mrs. Borg."

❖ try using the minimalist approach: "Sean, homework."

Instead of saying, "Don't come crying to me! I'm the one who told you not to hang out with Jennifer in the first place. I just knew this was going to happen. She's bad news."

❖ try allowing natural consequences. I'll tell you one thing, children never pick their friends according to our opinions. Want your kid to dump a bad influence? Tell him you like the friend so much you've asked him to bring over his adoption papers so you can sign them. Then, ask your kid if he minds moving into the broom closet so the friend can take over his room. Believe me, any kid you like is going to be history in terms of friendship.

All kidding aside, children soon learn how to choose their friends wisely. When they've associated with a variety of kids, all with different personalities, attitudes, values, likes and dislikes, and strengths and weaknesses, they gradually develop the ability to size up other children and decide whether the chemistry for a healthy friendship is there. But along the way, they're bound to attempt friendships that cause more grief than enjoyment. This natural consequence is an important steppingstone to choosing friends with whom they can have long-lasting, rewarding friendships. As you will see below, we can use open-ended questions to help children reflect on how to choose friends wisely and how to nurture those friendships that *are* worth keeping.

❖ try providing objective information: "It really hurts when good friends let us down."

❖ try using questioning: "What happened between you and Jennifer?" (When the child answers this question, she must stop reacting blindly to the situation and start introspecting. By making this switch, she begins to establish some real control over her problem instead of being at the mercy of her anger, disappointment, frustration, or sadness.) "What qualities did she have that made you want to be her friend?" (The child answers, reflecting on what qualities she seeks in a friend and whether those qualities truly predict a good friendship.) "What does she do or say that puts a strain on your friendship?" (The child answers, examining characteristics that would not, in her mind, qualify a person as a good friend.) "Do you think you can do anything to help her become a better friend?" (The child answers, contemplating her responsibility in the disagreement.) "What are you going to do about your friendship with her?" (When the child answers this question, she considers her options. Does she try to salvage the friendship by resolving their differences constructively, or does she cut her losses and move on?)

In each of these examples of alternatives, we encourage children to explore their own thoughts rather than pressuring them to adopt ours. Since these alternatives are nonconfrontational, they preserve adult-child harmony. By allowing kids to think for themselves, we tell them we have faith in them to either make the right choice or handle the consequences that are sure to rear their ugly heads when they make irresponsible ones. Eventually, children learn that the ability to recognize and control what shapes their choices is under their power and their power alone: one more giant step toward self-direction.

9

WORDS THAT
DOMINATE *and* CONTROL

*b*esides talking to children in a way that implies we're superior thinkers, we also exercise power over them in an effort to make them obey us. Some of the ways we do this are by delivering threats and ultimatums, unfair, degrading, or harsh punishments, and illogical punishments. Other domination and control tactics simply bar children from acting or speaking — placing them in a parentally imposed jail of sorts. These include our unreasonable denials, words we use to bring their conversation to a standstill, and words that forbid or discourage them from expressing certain feelings. Last, we often use phrases designed to wrest the truth out of them.

These kinds of controlling phrases are generally designed to make our lives easier by putting an end to any behavior we don't like, not to guide children to become responsible adults. While some are pretty direct, others are subtler. All, however, either offend children, erode their self-esteem, or both. Furthermore, since controlling phrases seldom address the reasons behind their misbehavior, they communicate that obedience is what counts, not the motives underlying the behavior. Now, let's explore each type of domination and control language and the healthier alternatives that command rather than demand good behavior.

Threats and Ultimatums

Fear is a powerful motivator in children, especially when its source is someone they love and respect. Short of physical punishments like spanking and hitting, nothing triggers more dread and worry in them than threats and ultimatums from adults. Examples might include the following:

❖ "Do as you're told, or I'll ground you for a month, and you'll never forget it." Most people don't like someone else telling them what to do or threatening them, and children are certainly no exception.

❖ "If you don't come inside right now, I'm going to take a switch to you!" Threats of physical punishment are highly effective in making children obey, but the force motivating them is a basic animal instinct: escaping pain.

❖ "This is your last chance. Either you act nicely to your classmates or I'm not going to let you play on the tire swing during recess for a month." What kid wants to be told they won't be able to do something for an entire month? Children don't like timed restrictions of any kind, so I bet if, instead of this ultimatum, the punishment was not being allowed to wash windows for a month, they'd still end up squealing in protest. You can probably consider not eating broccoli for a month a safe exception to this, though.

❖ "Because I'm the boss, that's why," is an implied threat. Sure, you and I know it's the fail-safe ploy we use when we have absolutely no idea what else to say, but it suggests that if children don't obey our wishes, we have full authority, as their supreme commanders, to make their lives miserable. It also tells them that whatever reasons we have are beyond their scope of understanding and that they aren't really worth the time and effort required to explain.

Clearly, some of these phrases can invoke enough anxiety to cause a lot of damage. Others lead our children to feel resentment and anger toward us. Some cause a little of both. So what substitutes can replace these threats and ultimatums?

Instead of saying, "Do as you're told, or I'll ground you for a month, and you'll never forget it" when your daughter ignores your requests to come to dinner,

* try giving an if/then limited choice: "If you come to dinner now, then you won't have to eat cold food later by yourself."

* If she doesn't respond to that choice, try rendering a logical consequence: "Dinner is over now, Sweetie. Next meal is breakfast," and stick to your guns no matter how loud the claims of starvation and the pleas for food.

* try questioning: "What's our rule about coming to the table when dinner is ready?" (The child answers, acknowledging the rule's existence.) "Why do you suppose we have that rule?" (The child answers, reflecting on the rule's purpose and the repercussions for having an open seating buffet line night after night.) "Good! So what do you need to do right now?" (The child answers, contemplating ways to be punctual when the call to dinner is sounded.)

Instead of saying, "If you don't come inside right now, I'm going to take a switch to you!"

❖ try the minimalist approach: "Michelle, inside, now."

❖ try using an "I" message: "I get very annoyed when my requests go ignored several times in a row."

❖ try giving a limited choice: "If you come inside when you're called, then you'll be able to play street hockey with your friends again tomorrow."

Instead of saying, "This is your last chance. Either you act nicely to your classmates or I'm not going to let you play on the tire swing during recess for a month,"

❖ try allowing a natural consequence: His classmates are not likely to let him get off easy. Some of them are probably not going to play with him for quite some time, making him feel lonely and left out. He'll learn that if he wants to have playmates, he needs to treat them nicely.

❖ try making an impartial observation followed by questioning: "You usually get along so well with your classmates. What's different today?" (The child answers, reflecting on factors that may have instigated his behavior toward his classmates.) "How could picking on your classmates affect you?" (When the child answers this, he reflects on how his behavior made him feel and the possible consequences he might experience in terms of his classmates' reactions.) "How do you suppose they feel when you treat them that way?" (The child answers, now reflecting on how he has affected others' feelings.) "How would you feel if you were treated the same way?" (The child answers, putting himself in the shoes of the classmates with whom he was at odds.) "What do you need to do to make things right?" (The child answers, considering ways to make things right with his classmates.)

❖ try giving a limited choice: "You can either get along nicely with your classmates or work on your project alone."

Instead of saying, "Because I'm the boss, that's why," when your teen questions why her curfew is one hour earlier than that of her friends the same age,

❖ try questioning: "What curfew do your friends have?" (The teen answers, either acknowledging the fact that she's not the only one with the same curfew or giving you the information you might use to extend her curfew if you decide it's appropriate.) "Other than your friends having a later curfew, what are some valid reasons for having your curfew extended?" (When the teen answers this question, she must test the soundness of her argument and come up with strong negotiating points.) Who knows? You might either come to a compromise or find her points valid enough to warrant changing her curfew.

❖ try using an "I" message that acknowledges both your feelings and hers: "I understand how frustrating it can be when some of your friends have curfew rules that are more lax. Nevertheless, there's been a lot of crime in the area lately. I love you, and I can't bear to see you get hurt."

❖ try making an impartial observation along with an "I" message: "There have been reports of gang activity in the area. Being caught in the crossfire of one of their turf battles could be fatal. I'm just not willing to take any chances with your safety."

Just like angry phrases, negative judgments, and shaming statements, threats and ultimatums make children comply because they fear our reaction — our anger, vengeance, or disapproval. Although they often work, these tactics are no substitute for teaching children to behave for the right reasons. If we want to guide them properly, we must *command,* not *demand,* their respect and attention.

Unfair, Degrading, or Harsh Punishments

Sometimes, it's difficult to decide just what kind of consequence children should experience for each type of misbehavior. Even if we're old pros when it comes to taking care of children, they can still surprise us by charting new territory in rule breaking.

As kids become preadolescents and teenagers, their misbehavior can get particularly creative, catapulting us into a whole new level of anxiety. In response, we're sent running frantically back to the drawing board to reinvent our discipline program. Suddenly time-outs don't work worth a hoot. Banishing them to their room is just what they want — it gives them a chance to crank the music up so loud that the mortar between the bricks loosens. And when we do discipline them in a way that catches their attention, they're quick to give us a detailed report on the customary discipline practices every other adult in the country uses. Naturally, all of them are much more lenient than ours.

But there are times when some adults cross the line and levy punishments that are either too harsh, degrading, or unfair. Sometimes they do so because the child has been committing the same offense over and over, week after week, until the adult is maxed-out in the frustration department. Ignoring it sure didn't make a dent. Idle threats just made the child giggle. So, the adult storms out of the corner he's been backed into and resorts to more drastic measures. I know one father who was so dismayed by his daughter's falling grades that every time she brought home a C or lower on her report card, he'd make her stay in her room, read an entire volume from the encyclopedia, and give an oral account to him afterward. The child was in third grade.

I know a mom who uses a lot of degrading punishments: she washes her children's mouths out with soap when they curse, talk back, or say unkind things to each other; and when they misbehave in other ways, she has them sit in a corner. All I can say is they must have the cleanest teeth in town, but when they grow up, I bet there won't be any rectangular rooms in their houses.

Sometimes, we're not sure if children are guilty of breaking a rule, so we play it safe with the "guilty until proven innocent" approach by levying a punishment just in case. To my mother, this was the "that's for what I didn't catch you doing" strategy. And darned if there wasn't always something I thought I had gotten away with scot-free. So much for dumb luck.

On occasion, our punishments are too rough, especially when we don't know what norms for "fair and reasonable punishments" other adults are following. Most of us are smart enough to know that a kid's accounting of those norms won't be accurate (particularly when they swear the usual and customary punishments include candy or later bedtimes). Sometimes our harshness springs from the fact that our own parents used the same punishment during the days of the autocratic family, and hey, we turned out just fine, didn't we?

When we punish in an unjust, degrading, or harsh way, the antagonism that results takes its toll on the harmony in our relationships with children. Sometimes, they wind up feeling so overwhelmed that they begin to think, "Who cares. I'm grounded for the rest of the year anyway. I can do anything I want, because what else can they really do to me?" There's always hope, though, for a better way. Let's look at some alternatives that will help us avoid resorting to such tactics:

Instead of levying a harsh punishment like, "That's it, you're grounded for a year" when your teen is caught cheating,

❖ try natural and logical consequences by making sure she gets a failing mark for the assignment and having her write a letter of apology to both the teacher and the class. She should also complete the assignment on her own for zero credit.

❖ try questioning: "What is the family rule about cheating?" (The teen answers.) "Why do you think that rule exists?" (The teen answers, reflecting on the rationale behind the rule.) "What are the long-term repercussions for your own life when you cheat?" (When the teen answers this question, he might reflect on the fact that, by cheating, he might just cheat himself out of an education.) "What effects might your cheating have on the rest of the class?" (The teen answers, reflecting on the consequences an "easy A" might have on those who prepared hard to earn their grade.) "How can your cheating affect your relationships with other people, including your classmates and teachers?" (When the teen answers this question, he must face the reality that cheating jeopardizes his reputation as a trustworthy person — a reputation that is much easier to lose than to earn back.) "How do you feel when someone you know cheats?" (The teen answers, reflecting on how unfair it is for someone to get a good grade by cheating while others struggle hard to earn that good grade.) "What can you do next time so you don't feel you have to cheat?" (The teen answers, contemplating strategies for being well prepared for any exam.)

❖ try providing objective information: "Students who cheat really cheat themselves of a good education, because the purpose of school is to learn, not to make good grades."

❖ try providing objective information that helps reinforce family rules and values: "We don't cheat in our family."

Instead of punishing unfairly with a statement like, "Since you drew all over the blackboard with markers, no recess for the whole class!"

❖ try logical consequences and objective information combined: "I want you to clean the board now. Vandalizing school property is against our rules. Furthermore, if these stains are permanent, it'll be difficult to see what's written on the blackboard."

❖ try using an "I" message and logical consequences combined: "I'm really sad that someone colored all over our classroom blackboard. It hurts me when people don't respect school property. I want it cleaned up right away. I'm putting the markers out of your reach until I feel you can be more responsible with them." Notice how this string of phrases focuses on the effect and solution rather than the blame.

Instead of using a degrading punishment like, "You're a very bad girl! Get the bar of soap so I can wash out that filthy mouth of yours!"

❖ try giving limited choices: "Either keep your language clean or leave the room so no one will be offended."

❖ try providing objective information: "People find bad words offensive."

❖ try the minimalist approach: Say the child's name to get her attention and pretend you're zipping up your mouth.

There are instances where groundings are appropriate. For instance, if your child goes somewhere with friends other than the promised destination and perhaps engages in behavior you don't allow, you may want to forbid him going out with friends for a certain period of time. But rather than arbitrarily defining that time yourself, as in, "No going out with your buddies for a month," make the kid earn back the privilege: "When I see that you're behaving more responsibly and are honest with me, you can have your social life back."

These alternatives are not only fair, but they also help children reflect on their choices, the repercussions, and solutions without provoking them to think what unreasonable tyrants we are.

Illogical Punishments

Adults impose illogical punishments for the same reasons they do unfair or harsh ones. And they often have similar effects on children — inciting anger and indignation that bring on a counter-attack that would make Napoleon look like Glenda, the Good Witch of the South.

Although a harsher illogical punishment may be more effective in bullying children to obey, when we do away with logic, the punishment makes no sense in the context of their misbehavior. How, then, can they produce the clear internal dialogue they need to feel remorse for their misbehavior and to keep from making the same mistake in the future? Even if, by some miracle, an illogical punishment does persuade them to think twice before repeating that same choice, chances are what's really motivating them is their desire to avoid punishment rather than their sense of right and wrong.

Just imagine a kid who is grounded for every instance of misbehavior. She's going to think, "I'd better not forget to take the clothes out of the washer, because I don't want to be grounded during the week of the eighth grade dance," rather than, "I don't want the clothes to get all mildewed so that I have to wash them all over again." How about a kid who thinks, "I better not stuff my hamster in my sister's pillowcase, because my dad will cream me," instead of, "... because Brownie might get smooshed, and my sister might get grossed out if she finds him"?

Here are some examples of phrases that deliver illogical punishments and examples of healthier alternatives that can replace them:

Instead of saying, "I want you to write 'I will not rip the heads off my sister's Barbie dolls' four hundred times on a sheet of paper,"

❖ try providing objective information and then deliver a logical consequence: "It's not nice to destroy other people's property. Get your wallet. I need to take you to the store so you can buy her a new Barbie doll."

❖ try questioning along with a logical consequence: "What's our rule about destroying someone else's property?" (The child answers, acknowledging that the rule exists.) "How do you think your sister feels?" (The child answers, pondering how her actions hurt her sister.) "How do you feel when someone breaks something of yours?" (The child answers, placing herself in the other person's shoes.) "What do you need to do to make things right between you and her?" (The child answers, reflecting on ways to make up for her wrongdoing.) Again, the logical consequence here would be for her to buy her sister a new doll with her allowance.

Instead of saying, "Your whining is driving me nuts. For that, you can't watch TV for a week,"

❖ try imposing a logical consequence: "I can't concentrate on my work with all this whining noise. I need you to go into the other room until you can speak in a normal voice."

❖ try giving a limited choice: "If you stop whining, we can go to the grocery store as we planned." Be sure you don't use choices as a bribe ("If you stop whining, I'll give you a treat") or threat ("If you don't stop whining, then I'm sending you to bed"). A when/then limited choice can also be used and might be phrased something like this: "When you can discuss your problem in a reasonable tone, then we can solve it and get on with our shopping."

❖ try using the minimalist approach: Say the child's name and give her that Mommy or Daddy look that could bring an evil villain to his knees.

Say you're a Boy Scout leader and one of the scouts breaks the cardinal rule not to walk with an open knife in his hands. Instead of saying, "That's not the behavior I'd expect in a good Boy Scout. Now I'm going to have to make you do the latrine cleanup duty for Josh,"

❖ try providing objective information and giving him a logical consequence: "It's not safe to walk around with an open knife. I need to take it from you until the trip is over."

❖ try using humor along with a logical consequence: "I guess you aspire to be a human shish kebab, Jack. Let me take that off your hands until you come up with a new goal."

When consequences make sense in terms of the misbehavior, children understand that they have no one else to blame but themselves. They can't blame us, because we haven't openly interfered. It's as though the logic surrounding the consequence they bring on themselves imparts a quality of inevitability to it — like a giant mudslide that sweeps them off their feet. We can stand aside, polish our halos with our shirtsleeves, and offer empathy, "Gee, I'm sorry, honey. I wish there were something I could do. These are the rules. I can't do anything to change them." (Quivering lower lip optional.)

Words That Control by Creating Obstacles

We can also control children by placing obstacles in their way. Since we're bigger, we essentially hold the keys to their lives, and (to the distress of teenagers everywhere) their cars. So, we have carte blanche to prevent them from doing what they want, whether those desires are unreasonable or reasonable. We can stop conversations with them in mid-sentence. We can set up road-blocks to their feelings. Why do we set up these barriers? To prevent kids from bulldozing their way through our lives like runaway trains, leaving only dust and rubble in their wake — in other words, to make our lives easier, at least in the here and now. But, since these obstacles lay the groundwork for poor self-esteem, resentment, emotional upheavals, and power struggles, as well as strengthening skills of manipulation and revenge, we have to pay the piper (or therapist) eventually. When it gets to that point, it's not a pretty sight, so it's better to avoid presenting kids with these obstacles in the first place. Let's look at the three most common adult-created obstacles.

Unreasonable Denials

From early on, kids constantly test their limits (and ours). As toddlers, they gleefully grasp at candle flames. As young children, they play barbershop with the sharpest pair of scissors in the house. As teenagers, they sneak into Uncle Larry's cigarettes to try their first smoke. Don't you get the impression that they chuckle in the face of danger while they do so? Since our job is to protect them from their own inexperience, we adults develop the uncanny ability to spew forth halts, denials, and refusals as fast as an Uzi gone haywire. When kids make requests that are dangerous, unde-served, or just plain impossible, these restrictions have their place — as long as they're accompanied by a logical explanation beyond the usual "because I said so, that's why." Besides, kids will nag you relentlessly if you don't explain. These explanations, when to the point and not condescending, can be our opportunity to impart valuable lessons. But there are many times when we reflexively say "no" without good reason: "No, you can't walk to the store. It's cloudy. What if there's a tornado?" "No, you can't play outside." "No, you can't go to the dance." "No, you can't go to the movies." "No, you can't help me cook." "No, you can't rearrange the furniture in your room." "No, you can't use the telephone." "No, you can't wear that shirt." No. No. No. No. No! I myself have uttered many an unreasonable denial based on one simple fact: I'm too lazy to think about what might happen if I say "yes." "Will I have to stop what I'm doing to drive them somewhere or get roped into helping them with their project?" Other times, I think, "Will they get themselves into some sort of trouble that will make me regret that three-letter word?" In my husband's mind, it's more like, "If I say "yes" now, will that open up the floodgates of their expectations that I've magically transformed into a pushover parent, thus paving the way to their becoming spoiled rotten?" Regardless of the motive, sometimes it's easier to say "no" than to say "yes." At least that's what we think when our vetoes roll reflexively off our tongues. Usually, however, children's annoying and long-winded responses prove us wrong.

Suppose that rather than heed our "nos," kids continue to beg and whine to get us to change (or lose) our minds. In this likely case, try using the "nevertheless" strategy. For instance, say you refuse to let your teenager go to Europe with two friends you don't quite trust. If he says, "But Dad, I'm sixteen years old!" reply with a statement that first acknowledges his feelings: "I know you're disappointed, especially since your friends are being allowed to go," then go in for the kill with the "nevertheless" part: "nevertheless, I don't feel comfortable with your traveling out of the country without adult supervision and with friends known to have gotten themselves into trouble in the past." If the kid persists, say the "nevertheless" part every time: "Nevertheless, I'm not comfortable letting you go," "Nevertheless, it doesn't feel right," and so on.

Eventually, he'll realize that you intend to stay firm despite his sighs of exasperation, and he'll accept your decision.

But when you stick that "Dead End" sign in front of their noses or erect those railroad-crossing arms in their paths without good cause or before giving them a chance to explain the details, then you're controlling children past what's reasonable. Children subjected to this often get angry and retaliate, shut down communication with you, or feel so powerless they stop reaching out in life.

So first stop and ask yourself questions like: "Is what he's asking reasonable?" "What's the worst that can happen if I say 'yes'?" "Is there an advantage to saying 'yes'?" "If I let him go through the experience, will he learn a valuable lesson, develop more independence, acquire or hone a skill, or improve his sense of self?" If we answer these questions honestly, many of those "nos" will turn into "yeses." Beware, though, if the child reads this paragraph, you may find him standing in front of you with these very questions scribbled on cue cards.

Communication Stoppers

I come from that era when grown-ups directed all adult-child communication like those people on aircraft carriers waving glowing sticks to direct fighter jets after they've landed on deck. But, instead of those sticks, they used phrases I'm sure you'll all recognize like, "End of discussion," or, "Period. Over and out!" These expressions were their attempts to bring the entire conversation to a screeching halt — usually a conversation the child was winning hands down. Sometimes, they'd use phrases that were intended to steer the discussion in their favor, not stop it altogether. Examples would include cutting a child off with an "I don't care" phrase: "I don't care. You're not going out with that bum!" The same effect can also be accomplished with "It doesn't matter," as in, "It doesn't matter what you say. I'm not going to change my mind and let you skip school tomorrow." In these cases, the adult may still be fool-ishly expecting an end to the griping and begging.

So, instead of cutting children off at the pass with our "I don't cares," "It doesn't matters," "End of discussions," and "Period. Over and outs," make sure you hear them out. If the conversation is going around in circles, and you are adamant about your posi-tion, you can try the "nevertheless" strategy mentioned in the preced-ing section. If there's half a chance either party will bend, you can say something like, "It doesn't seem like we're making any progress. Why don't we both sleep on it, and if either of us has anything new to bring to the table, we can talk about this tomorrow."

Another unproductive but surefire way to stop kids in their tracks is to say, "That's childish," or, "Stop acting like a child." Many adults are under the impression that children are supposed to act like miniature adults, so sometimes they say these phrases whenever a child acts silly, becomes a whirlwind of energy, or invites us to play. But to deny kids their childhoods is nothing short of criminal. In truth, it is we who should reclaim some of our childlike enthusiasm for life.

In our family, childishness is not only allowed, it's coveted, at least if the time and place are appropriate. Every time one of the kids asks an adult to join them in play, we never shrug it off as nonsense; we go along with them instead. I get on my hands and knees and play "horsey." My husband lets the girls put makeup on him and experiment with new hairstyles (although never with an overabundance of enthusiasm and always under the condition that all photographic equipment in the area be either banned or confiscated). We both play hide-and-seek, blindman's bluff, tag, and every other game to which I've forgotten all the rules. It's such a blast when we play together like this. Having children is a won-derful avenue for rediscovering your joie de vivre. Plus, without kids, how can we go to the latest Disney movie without getting peculiar looks and snickers? So, instead of saying, "Stop acting like a child," or "That's childish," try something like, "Hey, can I play?" "Whaddya wanna play next?" or "You sure look like you're having a blast!"

Obstacles to Expressing Feelings

Sometimes, we adults discourage children from expressing their feelings. From birth, kids are pros when it comes to letting the world know exactly how they feel. But over time, they get a metaphorical slap on the hand when they express good feelings beyond what others might consider appropriate or bad feelings, no matter what they might be. It's only natural that adults who were once on the receiving end of that slap should pass on to children their reluctance to express feelings freely. Furthermore, it's upsetting when the children we care about are sad, disappointed, angry, embarrassed, guilty, ashamed, or frustrated; I guess we hope that what isn't said isn't felt. But just what are displays of feelings designed to do? Some, like grief and disappointment, communicate to others our need for comfort. Others, like anger, embarrassment, and frustration, tell others to stop doing or saying whatever is bothering us. Displays of happiness and excitement show others what's making us feel good so we can share our joy and they can help us sustain it for as long as possible. Still others, like guilt and shame, are ways we communicate with ourselves so that we don't repeat the same mistakes.

When feelings are suppressed and harbored rather than felt and released, they're powerless as communication tools. Furthermore, when we cling to bad feelings, grudges form, which can grow and grow until they blow up in a four-megaton explosion that flattens everyone around it. When children are discouraged from expressing any feelings, good or bad, they feel self-conscious about receiving or giving expressions of emotions of any sort —

love, affection, frustration, disagreement, and so on. Here are some examples of phrases that suppress feelings and alternatives you can use instead:

Instead of saying, "Big girls don't cry,"

❖ acknowledge her feelings: "I'm so sorry your feelings are hurt. It's tough being picked on by older classmates."

❖ make sure she understands that tears can be healing: "Sometimes you feel better after you cry. It's a good way to release those feelings that are bothering you."

❖ offer a willing ear, not unsolicited advice: "If you need to talk, I'm here."

Instead of saying, "Snap out of it" when a child is sad,

❖ again, acknowledge his feelings and their appropriateness, then offer to listen: "I know how you feel. I'm sad about Wags dying, too. It's only natural that we feel grief right now. After all, he's been part of the family for fifteen years. We're all going to miss him so much. Do you want to talk about it?"

Instead of saying, "Stop acting like a maniac" when a child is overjoyed,

❖ let him revel in his happiness, unless it's not the right time or place. For instance, doing somersaults in the middle of a church service or dancing for joy in a five-star restaurant are not going to endear you or the child to the other people present. In these cases, you can say something like, "I'm thrilled you're so happy. Let's let it all hang loose and celebrate when we get home. Right now, we need to be quiet so we don't bother people around us."

❖ when the time and place are appropriate, acknowledge his feelings and the advantages of expressing them: "You're so happy now, and I'm just thrilled. It feels so good to let it all out, doesn't it? And when you act happy, you bring a smile to everyone else's face! It must be contagious."

Truth-Seeking Missions

Picture a secret agent in a dark room with a 500-watt bulb shining down and bamboo splinters and other torture instruments on a nearby tray. Behind the agent looms a hulking man with a thick accent warning him, "Vee have vays of making you talk."

Adults sometimes use similar tactics on children when they suspect or even know for certain that they're lying. But kids are good, really good. James Bond should be so tight-lipped. I don't think anyone, short of certified masters in torture with state-of-the-art equipment, could wrest a confession from some children. So when we say things like, "Did you spill this milk?" or, "Fess up. Which one of you shaved Fido with my razor?" they're just going to wind up feeling ashamed, angry, or scared — usually without spilling the beans. Furthermore, if the offense in question is pretty serious or if an innocent sibling winds up taking the rap unfairly, those truth-seeking missions can make a kid feel like an incorrigible criminal. What's worse, children who are habitually coerced into confessing learn to fear the truth and find better ways to cover their tracks.

Until kids are around six or seven, their lies are not very sophisticated. I remember when mine were little, they'd walk past me with their hands behind their backs saying something like, "Don't look, Mommy. I don't have a candy bar in my hands." They get a little older and their lies are only slightly less obvious: they start blaming their misbehavior and mistakes on the family pets. (Now you know why your kid keeps begging you to buy a dog.) A few years later, they start pointing their quivering fingers at their siblings. But when kids become teenagers, their conniving involves strategic planning that requires the cooperation of their friends and the comparing and contrasting of stories. You should start worrying when they start using cue cards and cheat sheets, spend hours practicing their best poker faces in front of the mirror, and begin recruiting undercover agents as alibis. The Pentagon should be so sophisticated!

What happens when we try to wring a confession from a kid who's actually telling the truth? As implausible as this may sound, it can actually happen from time to time. When my second youngest child, Lukas, was in kindergarten, he and another classmate were painting on easels draped with large sheets of white paper just outside the classroom door. After a while, his friend went back into the classroom to wash her hands. When the teacher went outside to check on Lukas, there he was, brush full of dripping paint standing right next to an elaborate painting — on the brick exterior of the school. Talk about getting caught with a smoking gun in your hand! The teacher insisted that Lukas confess. Over and over again, she demanded, "Tell the truth. I know you did it."

Eventually, he gave in and said he did. The teacher had him clean up the mess, and when I came to pick him up after school, she proclaimed, in a victorious tone reminiscent of Mohammad Ali's, how she had cleverly gotten the truth out of him. I asked Lukas what had happened, and he told me, "I really didn't do it, Mommy. Taylor did. I just had to go to the bathroom really bad, and so I told the teacher what she wanted me to say." Now, ten times out of nine (the new math), I'll take the teacher's word over my kids', but after overhearing Lukas on the telephone asking Taylor why she let him take the rap, I was certain he wasn't guilty. To top it off, he told me, "Santa Claus sees everything. At least *he* knows I'm telling the truth." The next morning, I fussed at his teacher for accusing him unjustly. Now that I'm older and (maybe) wiser, I know I should have let Lukas deal with the injustice on his own. After all, I can't rescue my children from all adversity, be it unfair or not. It would have been better to show Lukas I had faith in him to handle the incident on his own by acknowledging his feelings, giving him ample amounts of love and affection, and encouraging him to take care of the problem himself. I should have intervened only if he solicited my help after trying to handle things himself or if he began to shows signs that he couldn't handle it well, like balking at going to school, obsessing over the incident, and so on. What would I have done in the teacher's position? I would have said, "There's paint all over the wall. I would appreciate it if whoever was responsible for this would come forward. Otherwise, since both of you were out here painting, I expect both of you to clean this mess up. Whoever didn't paint the wall should have seen to it that the other one didn't either. We all take care of each other in this class." Look at the advantages to this approach:

❖ They both learn to extend their sense of responsibility beyond themselves instead of adopting an "everyone for themselves" attitude.

❖ The innocent party learns that sometimes life isn't fair. There will be times when he or she will get the blame for something they didn't do. When they experience injustice like this, it's an opportunity for them to learn how to assert themselves constructively and how to cope with frustration.

❖ When the innocent party is forced to be accountable for and clean up after someone else's poor choice, he'll undoubtedly feel resentment toward that person. Therefore, the responsible party will experience the natural consequence of having to deal with all that ire directed at him.

❖ Both kids learn to feel comfortable with the truth rather than to fear it as that "horrible monster that gets you into trouble."

❖ Both children learn to focus on the solution, not the blame.

We want children to respect the truth, not feel threatened by it. Those who perceive the truth as an evil menace are likely to become adults without a healthy and realistic sense of justice, adults who are afraid or unwilling to accept responsibility for their own mistakes. So, what can we say instead?

Instead of saying, "Did you spill this milk?"

❖ try making an impartial observation and providing objective information: "I see milk has been spilled on the table. When milk isn't cleaned up right away, it sours and gets really sticky." If they protest with, "But I didn't do it!" (and you know they did) you can counter with more objective information that reinforces those principles you want children to adopt in their lives: "In our family, we believe in being accountable for our mistakes," or "We believe in telling the truth in our family." If they still don't fess up, follow with, "I don't intend to focus on who's to blame. Since the important thing is to get this mess cleaned, I expect whoever made it to mop it up within the next few minutes." (Be sure not to hover silently, waiting to see who grabs the mop, as this is simply a nonverbal form of extorting the truth out of them.) By focusing on the solution rather than the blame, not only do we teach children to do the same, but we also avoid handing out accusations that can inflame the situation.

Say you're a grandparent and you have your two grandsons over for the weekend. Because they were roughhousing in the living room, your favorite Lladró figurine ended up in pieces.

First, let me say that any grandparent is taking a huge risk if they have breakables within reach of their younger grandkids — that's plain old Grandparenting 101. But if you learned this lesson the hard way, instead of saying, "Tell me which one of you did it, or you're both going home to your mom and dad now!"

❖ try providing objective information, making an impartial observation, and then — the coup de grâce — levying a logical consequence: "I see my favorite Lladró figurine is broken. As you both know, it's against my rules to roughhouse in this room. You can both save up enough money to replace it if you mow and edge the lawn, paint the exterior of the garage, and help with other odds and ends around here." (Little do they know how much Grandma's precious knickknacks cost. They'll both be working through college to pay off the breakage.)

❖ you can also use questioning and follow up with the same consequence: "What's Grandma's rule about doing outdoor activities inside? (The soon-to-be-impoverished children answer, acknowledging the existence of this time-honored rule.) "Why do you think that rule is important?" (The children answer, reflecting on the rule's purpose.) "What do you think is an appropriate consequence?" You'd be surprised how many kids will choose a harsh consequence. Nearly every child I interviewed responded, "I'll pay to have it replaced." Not one let themselves off easy with, "I shouldn't be allowed to take a bath or eat Brussels sprouts for a week." Amazing!

Instead of saying, "Fess up. Which one of you shaved Fido with my razor?"

❖ try imposing a consequence on anyone known to have been around the scene of the crime by saying, "Although it would show a great deal of courage for the person responsible to step forward and repair the damage. If no one is willing to do that, I don't wish to focus on who to blame. Since you both were in the room together with Fido, you can clean up this mess together and pitch in to buy me a new razor." Anyone who's innocent will naturally protest. You can then counter with, "If you didn't actually do it, it's your responsibility to help your brother resist turning the poor dog into a hairless wonder. It's not 'everyone for themselves' around here. We help each other stay out of trouble in our family."

This brings to mind a similar incident in my own house. One day, the kids rounded up all three of our dogs to play "doggie dentist." They borrowed my white doctor's coat, some of my medical equipment — fortunately only those things that were disposable, could be sterilized, or were broken anyway — and set up the big operation in one of their rooms. I heard all sorts of commotion up there — laughing, shouting important orders, and rolling around on the floor in hysterics — which, as you've probably guessed, wasn't coming from those poor dogs. Later that evening, I found my toothbrush and Waterpik missing from the bathroom. (Insert sound effects from *Psycho* here.) My biggest mistake wasn't pressuring the pilferer to confess; it was asking for what (and on whom) they had used my medical equipment. Ugh. What we don't know won't hurt us. On the bright side, I've never seen those dogs with whiter teeth!

When children *do* confess to something on their own, give them an "I" message that acknowledges this remarkable (and rare as chicken lips) internal achievement: "I admire the courage you showed by telling the truth. I know how difficult that can be sometimes, even for grown-ups." Structure your discipline so that children don't feel they're being punished for telling the truth. Simply having them correct their mistakes without giving them the third degree can prevent this misunderstanding. For example, they can clean their spills, pay for broken possessions, apologize for hurt feelings, and so on.

In short, phrases that dominate and control may be highly effective ways to make kids obey, but the seemingly positive results are almost always temporary. Instead of contemplating things like consequences, solutions, and healthier alternatives, they're going to be engrossed in thinking about how angry they are with us, how inadequate they feel, strategies for worming out of the punishment we've just imposed, ways they can be sneakier next time, or how they can take revenge. This all contributes to eroding whatever relationship we have with them.

As I mentioned before, we often resort to this form of adult-child communication because it preys on children's fear, a powerful emotion on which we sometimes capitalize in order to make our own lives easier. Fear of any sort is much more potent than logic in getting an externally directed person to do as we wish; fear of punishment, fear of losing, fear of anger, fear of disapproval, fear of not being loved, and fear of the truth are all external beacons that guide their choices. Furthermore, when we're busy tightening the thumbscrews, we aren't imparting any of the values and principles we want them to adopt. As Thomas Gordon wrote in his book, *Teaching Children Self-Discipline,* "The more you use power to try to control people, the less real influence you'll have on their lives."* The only things domination and control tactics inspire in children are revolt, blind conformity, or a more precise calculation of risk ("What are the chances of my getting caught?"). Without the proper set of values, with little or no practice

---

* Thomas Gordon, *Teaching Children Self-Discipline* (New York: Time Books, 1989), page 7.

exercising logic, and with no motivation to choose according to what's right, these children are loose cannons. Unleash them from our control, and they can't reason their way out of a wet paper bag. So we must either keep a tight rein on them the rest of their lives or turn them loose and hope they (and everyone they meet) survive. After all, we can't supervise them until they're ninety, can we? I shudder at the thought.

On the other hand, if we encourage self-direction in children, they'll be motivated by reason, not fear. They'll feel free to consider their problems from an objective viewpoint rather than rely on outside evaluations. So we must ask ourselves: do we want children to make the right choices because they're afraid of what we might do or say if they don't, or do we want them to make the right choices for the right reasons, even when no one is watching? After all, the pot of gold at the end of the rainbow is for them to become responsible adults, not for us to travel the path of least resistance.

IO

WORDS THAT HINDER
REASONING *and* INDEPENDENCE

*M*any of the phrases we've already covered not only encourage approval seeking in children, but they also steer them from delving deep into their choices to analyze them. Kids are great at picking the lint out of their belly buttons strand by strand. They're pros at examining their noses for boogers to decide which are edible and which deserve to be relegated to the undersurface of a table. But for some reason, their brains lack what their fingers possess: the ability to take apart a past or potential choice component by component to determine if it's in agreement with their values, if any of their past experiences color it one way or another, if it has any consequences — good or bad — for themselves or others, if it carries any advantages or disadvantages, and if there might be better alternatives to choose.

Kids need to exercise their reasoning muscles to come anywhere close to the dexterity of those persistent and discriminating fingers. But, many times what we say prevents them from doing that. We've already covered those phrases that have a judgmental quality. And there are those that encourage them to respond out of fear of our reaction, like angry remarks and threats. There are also the ones with a push-button effect — "stop," "no," "don't," "can't," and "quit" — which provoke a reaction that brings Pavlov's slobbering dog to mind. And what about those that tell children they aren't able to make good choices without us? All these silence that little voice inside that's supposed to help them reflect on each decision, opinion, and idea. But these phrases are just the tip of the iceberg; there are many more where they come from. Specifically, there are those that, though they don't pass judgment, nevertheless hinder the development of reasoning and encourage them to be dependent on us.

Words That Hinder Reasoning

Of all the harmful phrases we use in our adult-child communication, those hindering the development of children's reasoning skills are the most deceptively benign. Most of them don't appear the least bit harsh, and many even seem compassionate and loving. Yet, they can be among the most harmful for two reasons: First, they undermine children's confidence by sending them the message that we don't have faith in them to think for themselves. And if *we* — the people who love them most — don't, then why should they? Second, these phrases rob children of the crucial skills they need to live successfully as adults: the ability to make responsible choices, the ability to resolve conflicts and other problems, the ability to face challenges, and the ability to overcome adversity — all essential to self-reliance, self-confidence, integrity, and, therefore, happiness.

Let's first take a look at what I call "directives."

Directives

Since children are born into this world knowing little other than how to cry, fart, burp, drool, poop, pee, wiggle, and make cute gurgling sounds, it seems a given that we, as their guides, are there to tell them what to do to expand their abilities beyond these charming talents. I, for one, had built a life centered around what seemed like my God-given right as an adult, spending nearly every waking moment telling my children what to do. Sadly for my husband, this inclination often spilled over onto him. I still struggle to resist the urge to give orders, because deep down, I, like other adults who care for children, feel better equipped to live their lives for them. I mean, what if I (gulp) *did* let them fend for themselves? They might mess up, scarring their self-esteem for life or, at the very least, throwing a monkey wrench into my tightly scheduled day.

When you think about it, we usually don't tell other adults what to do. If I were to say to my friend Kathy, "Go wash your hands before supper," she'd probably hurl me a look that could make me curl into a fetal position and suck my thumb. However, if I were to play a tape recording from a few years ago of a typical conversation with my five kids, it would probably go something like this: "Erik, go get your jacket on. Kristina, come down for supper. Annika, start your homework. Lukas, pack your lunch for school. Michelle, feed the dogs. Do your chores, kids...." Only a frayed thread of sanity prevented me from telling them when to breathe, fart, belch, pick their noses, or scratch an itch.

Some of my directives were pretty benign, because I would say them so nicely that my kids, on a superficial level, felt they weren't in any danger of punishment if they ignored me, but they all knew, deep down, that things could escalate if they did. The examples I just mentioned would belong to this "warm and fuzzy" directive category. Those I voiced in anger were a bit more threatening. Examples of these "you'd better watch out" directives include some we've already covered in the section in chapter 4 on angry words: "Put that back!" "Keep your hands to yourself," "Control yourself!" and so on.

Did my directives work the way I wanted them to? Actually, thanks to an occasional miracle, my kids sometimes complied, but they did so as a push-button, automatic response or as a reaction to the looming threat of incurring the wrath of the Mommy Monster. Many times, they wouldn't follow my directives exactly as I had hoped, because verbal commands tend to have more gaps and leave more room for misunderstanding than phrases that stimulate a child to do his or her own reasoning.

For instance, when my son Erik was four, he used to love to cavort about naked. One day, when we were entertaining relatives from Norway in our backyard, Erik was having the time of his life chasing his sisters on his tricycle with nothing on but his birthday suit to protect him from things like spokes, handlebars, and tire treads. Since I had hopes of him providing me with several grandchildren, I told him, "Erik, go inside and get dressed." He did go inside, and, after five or ten minutes, came back dressed — in only his cowboy boots. I guess one man's idea of fully clothed is another man's idea of overkill.

Most of the time, however, my kids would reply to my directives by sighing, groaning, looking exasperated, or using some other well-practiced signal to let me know I was being an annoying nag. So what can we say to replace our directives? For one, most directives can be softened when prefaced with, "I would like you to..." "I need you to..." "Would you mind..." or "Could you please...." After all, this is usually how you would introduce a request to another adult. However, you should never use "Would you mind..." or "Could you please..." when trying to get a child to carry out a responsibility, to stop misbehaving, or to do something else that's mandatory, not optional. We'll discuss this in greater detail later on. Meanwhile, let's examine other healthier alternatives to directives:

Instead of, "Erik, go get your jacket on,"

❖ try making an impartial observation and then follow up with questioning: "Erik, it's twenty degrees outside. What do you need to do to make sure you're warm enough at recess today?"

❖ try giving a logical consequence: Let him go to school without a jacket, but call the teacher to say, "Erik neglected to wear his jacket to school, so he won't be able to play at recess. I don't want him getting sick. If you want him to catch up on any schoolwork or work on areas he needs extra practice in, maybe he can stay in the classroom and do that instead." (Kids are crazy about this one.)

❖ try giving a limited choice: "I will be able to take you to school as soon as you're dressed for this cold snap."

Instead of, "Annika, start your homework,"

❖ try making an impartial observation: "I see it's almost suppertime and you haven't started your homework yet."

❖ try using the minimalist approach: "Annika, homework."

❖ try using natural consequences: If she doesn't get her homework done, she'll have to contend with whatever consequence her teacher delivers.

Instead of saying, "Lukas, pack your lunch for school tomorrow,"

❖ try using the minimalist approach: "Lukas, lunch."

❖ try allowing a natural consequence: If he doesn't pack his lunch, he'll be awfully hungry the next day.

❖ try using humor: Stick a Post-it note on his empty lunch box that says, "Help! I'm starving to death! Please feed me before I waste away to nothing."

❖ try giving a limited choice: "When you've finished packing you lunch for school, then you can go outside and play with your brothers and sisters," or, "What would you like to do first, pack your lunch or go over your spelling words?"

Instead of saying, "Tommy, get back to your seat this instant,"

❖ try giving a limited choice: "When you're seated at your desk, then I can continue reading this book to the class." At this point, his classmates will probably impose a natural consequence — griping at him until he sits. This may not be the case, however, if a pop quiz or spelling test is involved.

❖ try providing objective information: "It's difficult for everyone in the class to pay attention to what I'm reading when someone is wandering around the room."

As you can see, the healthier alternatives to directives make it easy for children to think about their choices because they don't attack their pride. When they're able to think for themselves in this way, they will be well along on the path toward self-direction. On the other hand, directives, unkind or benign, either put children on cruise control by doing the thinking for them or elicit thoughts that have nothing to do with reflecting on and solving the problem, thoughts about what nags we are or what rotten kids they are. In all cases, directives foster external direction, because when we tell children exactly what choices to make, we become the external beacons that allow them to bypass introspection altogether.

Bailout Phrases

During my "greenhorn mommy" years, I don't think a day went by that I didn't let my kids off the hook for something. Having five of the little boogers made time a precious commodity that often hurled the entire household into a state of frenzy. Carrying through on my threats, getting them to pick up after themselves, hoping they would do their chores without being told twenty-seven times, and watching my toddler fumble with his shoelaces while I hovered over him, biting my tongue and tapping my foot, seemed to be luxuries for which I had little time or patience. No, I was into getting a quick fix. There was no way I was going to be late taking them to school or ballet practice; no way I was going to move "return videos to Blockbuster" and "clip kids' toenails" to the next day on my PalmPilot; no way I was going to be inconvenienced by their inexperience and risk trashing my reputation as the Martha Stewart of the mommy world. But first and foremost, I picked up the slack because I didn't want to hurt, inconvenience, or upset my own kids. I just loved them too much to see them squirm.

So, to spare my kids and me that kind of grief, I became "bailout queen" for the entire family. Being the control freak that I am, this came to me quite easily. I did their chores if they didn't respond to my first request (not without some major complaining, of course). I didn't punish them if they misbehaved at home or school. I wiped up their spills rather than waiting for them to do it. I intervened at the first sign of struggle, no matter what the task. I even helped my children more than I should have with their book reports. (One's in the running for the Pulitzer Prize. I'm so proud.) Well, you get the picture. I basically lived their lives for them. It was much easier for me because, hey, I was so much better at it than they were. Some of the things I'd say included rescue phrases like "Here, let me tie your shoes for you," "If you can't come up with anything to write, I'll do the next five sentences for you," and "Give me the rag. I'll take care of that spill." Other phrases were excuse promoters that helped them justify their mistakes, such as, "You didn't mean to do it," "It doesn't matter," or "You couldn't help it."

The problem with my maternalism gone awry was that I would constantly reach the point of being overwhelmed. Once there, I'd either go on a "don't mess with mommy" rampage or give Joan of Arc a run for her money with my "I'm sick and tired of being the only one who does anything around this house" schtick. But how on earth could they fulfill their responsibilities when I'd always beat them to the punch? Not only that, whenever I bailed them out of a task or challenge, I denied them the chance to acquire new skills and overcome difficulties on their own. Why would they bother trying? They were rescued from consequences, frustration, boredom, responsibilities, commitment, hardships, and conflicts. In other words, they had their own personal slave, butler, and whipping boy — me. In truth, I wasn't really rescuing them at all, because to shelter them from trials and tribulations is to rob them of life itself. How much fun could that be? Kids who are constantly rescued become helpless. Their sense of dependency soon chips away at their self-esteem until feelings of inadequacy weigh them down. In the end, they become demanding adults with a bloated sense of entitlement.

Eventually, I came to my senses. I'm not sure exactly when reality slapped me in the face. Perhaps it was when my five-year-old hollered out, for the umpteenth time, "Mooooommmmmmmm! Come and wipe my butt." I guess that's where my maternal instincts drew the line.

So what would I say today, now that I've abdicated my throne as the bailout queen? Here are some examples:

Instead of saying, "Here, let me tie your shoes for you,"

❖ let them try their best, offering help only when solicited. I personally don't accept "I can't do it" from my kids (more on this later in the chapter). Instead, I encourage them to say, "I need some help, please, Mommy," before I'll lend a hand. Even if they fail, I still try to point out what they did well in the task: "You tie a mean square knot. You've really mastered that part."

Instead of saying, "If you can't come up with anything to write, I'll do the next five sentences for you,"

❖ let them do their work on their own. If my kids ask for suggestions, of course I'll offer some, in general terms, but I never lay a finger on their homework anymore. When they get a good grade, they know it's theirs, not mine. After all, I already passed fourth grade once, and I see no point in doing it again.

❖ offer impartial observations followed by questioning when the child does complete an assignment on his own: "I noticed you did your whole book report without begging for me to help once! What did you find easier and quicker, just biting the bullet and doing it on your own or begging first, then sitting down to do it yourself anyway?" (When the child answers this question, he may come to realize that preceding the assignment with futile solicitations for help just needlessly drags out the agony.) "How do you feel about accomplishing something on your own compared to having someone do part of the work for you?" (The child answers, reflecting on how proud he is when he completes a project independently.)

❖ if they whine and balk, try using an "I" message: "I have faith in you to do this on your own."

❖ try providing objective information: "Parents aren't allowed to do their children's book reports."

❖ you could also try giving a logical consequence in the form of a limited choice: "When you've completed your assignment, then you can go outside and play with your brothers and sisters."

❖ natural consequences can also guide a child in this case: If she doesn't complete the assignment on her own, she'll receive poor marks as well as other consequences from her teacher, like having to do the assignment during class, at recess, or after school.

Instead of saying, "Give me the rag. I'll take care of that spill,"

❖ try making an impartial observation followed by questioning: "I see you've spilled the milk. What do you need to do now?" Again, if my child were new to the task, I'd try to point out the parts she was successful in: "You got the milk carton and your cup out by yourself! Now you can take this rag and clean up the milk that didn't make it into your cup."

❖ limited choices would work well here, too: "You can have a fresh glass as soon as you've cleaned up this spill."

❖ you could also try using the minimalist approach by just pointing at the spill, looking expectantly at the child, and saying, "Sammy, milk."

Instead of saying, "You didn't mean to do it," when a child knocks over a table lamp with his baseball,

❖ try providing objective information: "Playing ball is an outdoor activity, not an indoor one." Then make sure he suffers a logical consequence: "I will need to deduct $47 from your allowance to replace the lamp."

❖ try using questioning along with that same consequence: "What's our rule about playing ball inside the house?" (The child answers, remembering the rule.) "Why do we have that rule?" (The child answers, reflecting on the rule's rationale.) "Good. So what do you need to do to make things right?" (The child answers, coming up with ways to make amends. At the very least, this might include giving an apology and earning the money to pay for another lamp.)

More often than not, we don't have to make excuses for children because they master that skill soon after birth. But, as discussed before, when they come up with one, like, "I couldn't help it," or, "He hit me first," focus on the solution rather than the blame. For example, say, "I'm not interested in excuses. I want a solution to the problem," or, "If we make other people respon-sible for our problems, then what control do we really have over them or over life itself? It's better to take responsibility for our choices and feel a little guilty than be a victim, under someone else's control."

The first several weeks after I stopped rescuing my children from everything, they weren't exactly thrilled with the change and would tell me what a mean mommy I was — a perfect opportunity for me to use humor in my response by calmly saying, "I know. That's my job," because it really is! Our ultimate goal is to work ourselves out of the job of doing everything for our kids. Being their guides should be a role we phase out over time. All in all, my transformation from bailout queen to evil mother has made my job easier in the long run. What's more, within several weeks of abdicating my throne, my children seemed happier and more confident about themselves.

I now know I'm doing all I can to raise my children to be responsible, moral adults, and there's no greater gift a mother can give her children. I cringe when I watch some of my friends reap the questionable rewards of their bailout tendencies. Sure, their kids cling to them like flies on flypaper, but the lives of their parents gives the term "labor-intensive" a whole new meaning. One mom still cuts up her sixth grader's chicken tenders. Another carries her 120-pound fifth grader around whenever the kid's tired. I don't know about you, but my day is already filled with enough hard labor.

Words That Encourage Helplessness

Adults unwittingly take the wind out of children's sails. Instead of encouraging them to spread their wings and try, we either caution them to keep their feet on the ground or clip their wings. It's scary to see kids stumble and fall. It's time-consuming to stand by and wait while they fumble with a new skill. It's annoying to hear their whines of frustration. So, we say things that stop their progress with phrases like the following:

"You're Too Little" Phrases

I truly believe children come into this world thinking they're faster than a locomotive and capable of leaping tall buildings in a single bound. But, we adults (think we) know differently. A few years under our belts have made it clear that there are lots of things *we* can't do (just don't dare let *that* cat out of the bag!). When I was five or six, I would spend hours jumping off our air conditioner compressor, absolutely certain I could learn how to fly given enough time and practice. But, after a few lumps and bruises, it became clear soaring with the eagles wasn't in the cards for me.

When we see this feeling of omnipotence in kids or their desire to take on something we think they're not ready to handle, we intercede. Why? Because if it's something that truly needs to be done, like a toddler learning to button a shirt or fix his own breakfast, it might take forever for him to realize he needs help. That means more watch-glancing and foot-tapping for us, which is a problem if time is a precious commodity. It also means more work for us cleaning the meses they leave behind, quelling our own fears that they might get hurt, and licking their wounds of frustration when they don't succeed. So, to spare the child and ourselves, we often say things like, "You're much too little to make oatmeal on your own," "You're too young to play football with the other kids," "I don't think you're ready to sleep without Pull-Ups yet," and, "You're only twelve, guys! If I let you go hiking alone, there's no way you'd find your way. You'd be bear-bait in no time."

These phrases often make children feel inferior. Not only will they start believing they're incompetent in that activity or task, but they also start doubting their own judgment. In time, they delegate the more difficult tasks to others, even those they could eventually accomplish with time and practice. In some children, statements like these create ill feelings like resentment and anger. What's more, any combination of these feelings detracts from thinking about what must be done to complete a task and whether, given their strengths, weaknesses, and experience level, they can do so alone, with help, or not at all. Children must learn to figure these things out on their own. Otherwise, they may become adolescents and adults who don't have a realistic conception of what they can and cannot do. They either underachieve or engage in high-risk behavior that's dangerous. For instance, if I had never been allowed to let my lumps and bruises teach me that no amount of arm flapping would make me airborne, who knows? I might have taken a leap from the Empire State Building with a set of homemade wings instead of letting my fingers do all the flying —over this keyboard.

In the case of situations where it's truly unsafe for children to do something beyond what's appropriate for their age, size, or experience level, they deserve a reasonable explanation rather than an unmitigated verdict. Let's take a peek at some thought-provoking alternatives to the examples I mentioned earlier:

Instead of saying, "You're too young to play football with the other kids,"

❖ try providing objective information: "Sports experts generally agree that kids should not play football until they're eleven or twelve."

❖ try using an "I" message followed by questioning: "I'm afraid you're going to get seriously injured if you play football with kids twice your age. What do you think could happen if you get tackled by a guy bigger than you?" (The child answers, considering the repercussions of experiencing Newton's Law firsthand.) "How do you suppose you'd feel if you broke an arm or a leg?" (The child answers again, reflecting on the consequences an injury would have on his mobility, his performance at school, and so on.) "What do you think breaking an arm or a leg would do to the rest of your summer?" (The child answers, thinking about how such an injury would spoil a huge chunk of his summer vacation.) "Do you know of any sports you might be interested in where size is not that important?" (The child answers, considering safer options.)

❖ try giving a limited choice in combination with an "I" message: "I feel uncomfortable with your playing football with boys twice your size. I see Chapelwood is offering karate classes and baseball camp. Would one of those interest you?"

Instead of saying, "You're much too little to make oatmeal on your own,"

❖ let the child try, and help only when he asks you to. You can use impartial observations to point out what he did well in the task: "You added exactly the amount of water the instructions called for. And look, you didn't spill a single drop of milk."

❖ or offer guidance by means of questioning: "What do you need to cook the oatmeal in?" "What do you need to do first?" "How much water do you need to add?" "How many minutes do you need to cook it for?" "Now that it's cooked, what do you need to add to the bowl?" (When the child answers these questions, he must either refer to the directions or ask our advice. He also might realize that cooking is more complex than it appears. It requires preparation, the ability to tell time or use a timer, the ability to use measuring cups or spoons, and the ability to read directions.)

Make sure the child handles any consequences — cleaning the dishes afterward, mopping up spills, putting away packages, throwing away trash, et cetera.

Instead of saying, "I don't think you're ready to sleep without Pull-Ups yet,"

❖ try delivering a logical consequence: Make sure if the child wets his bed, he helps you strip and wash the bedding. But remember to deliver the consequence in a nonthreatening, respectful way so the child doesn't feel ashamed or afraid.

❖ try giving a limited choice: "When you have three dry nights in a row, then we can try without Pull-Ups."

❖ try making an impartial observation, then following it with questioning: "You have had dry Pull-Ups seven nights in a row, so we can try wearing regular underwear if you want. What things can you do to give yourself a better chance of staying dry all night?" (The child answers, considering strategies like not drinking fluids after a certain hour, being sure to empty his bladder before going to bed, etc.) "If you have an accident, what do you need to do?" (The child answers, reflecting on how he must take responsibility for his mistakes, even those that are unintentional. If he's old enough, he'll be able to list the steps required to clean up after an accident, including changing the sheets, changing his clothes, doing laundry with or without help, et cetera.)

If you're a camp counselor and two of the campers beg to hike alone in the forest, instead of saying, "You're only twelve, guys! If I let you go hiking alone, there's no way you'd find your way. You'd be bear-bait in no time,"

❖ try making an impartial observation, providing objective information, and following up with a limited choice: "You've both learned a great deal of wilderness skills this week. Nevertheless, there are many skills I haven't taught that are important to survival. Those skills take months, not weeks, to learn. If you can get the other campers to agree and we can get the preparations done, we can plan an overnight hike together by the end of the week."

❖ try using an "I" message: "It took me more than six months of intense training to be confident I wouldn't get lost, starve, or be eaten out there. I'd be reckless and irresponsible to allow you to go it alone after just one week out here."

❖ try using humor: "Sure thing! Those mountain lions have been looking pretty scrawny, so I'm sure they'd be grateful for a little appetizer." (If they respond by packing their backpacks and waving their good-byes, you can use one of the above alternatives to make sure they aren't part of some carnivore's seven-course meal.)

Unless it's dangerous, children should try to do as many things on their own as they can. Their attempts not only give them the opportunity to learn a new skill, but they also teach them that there are consequences — good and bad — to task-related choices. In addition, they let children explore their limits and potential, teaching them to cope with frustration and defeat, therefore fostering perseverance. Regardless of success or defeat, exploring life's experiences within safe limits is crucial to developing a secure sense of self.

Words of Pessimism

Pessimistic phrases are often the deterrents we adults use when we're afraid children can't manage a task easily — whether our intention is to make their lives easier or ours. We're quick with statements that reflect our lack of faith in their ability — statements like, "That won't work," "You won't be able to do that," "You can't reach that," and "That's too hard for you." But, unless a task is dangerous, there's no room for discouragement in adult-child communication, because it sends the harmful message that we don't have faith in children. Let's take a look at some pessimistic phrases and the healthier alternatives that encourage independence:

❖ Instead of saying, "That won't work," either let them figure that out on their own (they may prove you wrong), or say, "Hey, it's worth a try, Buddy. Go for it. I'm behind you all the way!"

❖ Instead of saying, "You can't do that by yourself," try saying, "Let me know if there's anything I can do to help you."

❖ Instead of saying, "You won't be able to reach/lift that," try saying, "I'll be glad to help you lift/reach that if you like."

We should discourage pessimistic statements from kids, too. When mine say, "I can't do it," I encourage them by saying, "Maybe you can. It's worth a try," or I model the words they could say instead, words that don't convey a lack of faith in themselves, like, "Can I have some help?"

One of the best ways to foster independence is by making children feel needed. Everyone wants to contribute in some way, and kids are no exception. So, even when I don't need their help (and deep inside prefer not to have it), I make a sincere request like, "Honey, my earring fell behind the couch, and my hands are too big to reach it. Would you mind giving it a try?" or, "I know it's not your chore today, but I'm so overwhelmed with getting dinner ready, I'd really appreciate it if you would set the table for me." Afterward, I reinforce how important they are as a contributing member of the family or the group: "Thanks. I don't know what I'd do without you."

Compare this approach with making children accomplish something because it's good for them: "You need to learn how to pitch in. Set the table," or, "It's good for you to learn to be responsible and hardworking, so once you finish washing the dishes, I want you to take out the trash." Kids aren't nearly as eager to do something when it's a duty, obligation, or learning experience as they are when they feel needed.

Words That Foster Failure-Phobia and Dependency

Many adultisms encourage or perpetuate children's fear of failure. When they're afraid to fail, they're afraid to try. When they don't try, they become stagnant and stop growing. This robs them of the very essence of childhood. There are ways to encourage a healthy attitude about mistakes and failures and to endow kids with sound defeat-recovery skills. Let's look at several categories of phrases that promote failure-phobia and dependency, as well as their healthier replacements:

Resist taking over for children when they struggle.

Instead of saying, "Let me do that for you," take the time to encourage them along the way with phrases like, "You're almost there!" "I know you can do it!" and "I know it's hard, but it looks like you're very close." We all learn through struggle more than observation, especially if that struggle is accompanied by encouragement from the cheerleaders on the sidelines.

Respond to their requests for help with limited assistance.

If children ask for help when they clearly haven't given it the good old college try, with appeals like, "Mom, can you help me?" and "I'm stuck. Do it for me, Daddy," you might say, "Let's see what you can do by yourself first, then we'll do together the parts you can't finish," or "I'll help you as soon as I see you've tried your best to do it on your own."

Encourage accountability.

When children fail, they should feel safe claiming ownership of that failure if they're to experience and learn from it fully. When we say things like, "It's all right. It's not your fault," or if they overhear us say things to other people like, "He couldn't help it," we send the message that we're eager to absolve them from responsibility for their every mistake. Consequently, children begin to see defeat as such a horrible proposition that to take the blame for it would be too painful to bear. Otherwise, why would adults, whose role is frequently to protect them from any discomfort, swoop in on their white steeds like knights in shining armor to spare them the burden that often comes with full accountability? So, instead of making excuses for children's failures, help them see the silver lining in each setback, as in the following examples:

❖ Instead of saying, "Jay, it's not your fault that Ryan got his feelings hurt. He had no business eavesdropping on you and Ben making fun of his speech impediment," you can first acknowledge his embarrassment by saying, "Jay, I understand how uncomfortable you feel, considering Ryan's always been a close friend of yours. I'm sorry you're in this awkward predicament." Then, help him reflect on the situation and its solutions with a series of open-ended questions: "What risks, if any, are there to discussing a person behind his or her back?" (Jay answers, reflecting on those risks.) "When one of your friends gossips about others, how does that make you feel about your friend's character? Would you feel confident that he wouldn't talk about *you* behind your back?" (When Jay answers these questions, he thinks about how he regards gossipmongers in general, and he considers how he'd feel to find out he had been gossiped about.) "You and Ryan have been friends for five or six years. How do you plan to repair the damage that's been done?" (Jay answers, reflecting on the importance of that friendship and what he can do to salvage it.)

❖ Instead of saying, "It's all right. You couldn't help it," when your daughter loses the jacket you bought her a month earlier, try acknowledging her feelings with an impartial observation: "You seem so disappointed about your jacket. I remember you saying it was one of your favorites." Then provide objective information and a logical consequence: "Everyone loses things from time to time. Since you labeled it with your name, it may turn up in the lost and found eventually. If not, you will have to earn the money to buy a new one. Maybe you can babysit kids in the neighborhood, start a dog walking service, or do other odd jobs here and there. I know you'll come up with some ingenious money-making idea as you have so many times in the past."

Encourage, encourage, encourage.

Encourage children to take on and persevere in new challenges they have a reasonable chance of mastering. In fact, encourage them to take on ones they might fail in as well, as long as you think they don't have a strong emotional attachment to success in that endeavor. For instance, my youngest daughter, Annika, wanted to take ballet lessons with her best friend, Brianna, when they were both around six or seven years old. Annika's attention span, however, was extremely short for her age, so I knew it would be difficult for her to pay attention to the instructor. Nevertheless, I encouraged her to take the class. Sure enough, while the other girls listened attentively, Annika was doing her own moves at the bar, facing the other direction, and admiring herself in the mirror, tutu and all. Sometimes, she'd take off for the middle of the room and do her own variation of *Swan Lake*. She got fussed at a number of times but could never focus for long. With my encouragement, she kept going to the class because she enjoyed the company of her friends and didn't really have her hopes set on being the next Anna Pavlova. In the end, she was proud of what she had accomplished and how she had persevered despite the challenge and the fussing.

Encourage children to practice their emerging skills as well: "You haven't practiced learning to ride your bike all week. It's going to be difficult to ride without training wheels when your bike is sitting in the garage gathering dust. If you get your helmet now, I'll be glad to help you. If we both work together, you'll be riding like a pro before the weekend."

Other phrases can inspire children to rebound from defeat, to risk making mistakes or failing at something, and to courageously overcome the obstacles that stand between them and independence. Here are some examples:

❖ "I'm so grateful for all of my failures. I've learned so much more from them than from my successes."

❖ "All the great people in history had to make many mistakes to accomplish what they did."

❖ "It's completely okay to make a mistake or fail at something as long as you turn that mistake or failure into an opportunity to learn something valuable."

❖ "I admire the courage you showed in taking on such a challenge. Even though things didn't work out entirely as you wanted, your effort and perseverance reveal a lot of inner strength."

In our family, we like to have mistake contests every Friday where, during dinner, we share the mistakes we've made during the week. When each person has finished recounting their blunders out loud, we all vote on those we believe offered the most valuable learning opportunities.

Point out the successes in every failure.

To have a healthy attitude about mistakes and failure, children must see them as stepping-stones to success, not weapons of self-destruction. We can help them internalize this attitude when:

❖ we value their having tried instead of focusing only on the outcome: "You really put your all into the driving lesson today. I admire your courage. Sure you ran up a few curbs [okay, so she trenched three front yards], but you didn't give up. Come back for your lesson tomorrow, and I bet with your level of determination, you'll be giving Mario Andretti a run for his money before long."

❖ we show them the successes within the failure: "I know you're disappointed about not getting into the journalism class, but all your practice taking photographs and writing newspaper articles has paid off. You've had a chance to show what a creative eye you have, plus your writing in composition class seems more confident and expressive."

❖ we point out the value of mistakes: "You may be disappointed that you wrote a report on the wrong subject, but you did learn the importance of making sure you understand instructions. And the paper you did on Benjamin Franklin was detailed and well written. I'm sure there'll be an opportunity for you to use it for a future assignment. Plus, you know a lot more about the guy now than you did before!"

Give objective feedback for their successes.

The last thing kids need when they make a mistake or fail is an adult rubbing their noses in it. There is no place for criticism, reprimands, ridicule, shame, or other indications that we're disappointed in them. What they need instead is our objective feedback, encouragement, empathy, and acknowledgment of their feelings.

Sometimes children need a tap on the shoulder so they can see and appreciate the progress they've made as well as the effort, courage, and perseverance it took them to do so. "Two months ago, you didn't know how to put on your rollerblades. Now look at you — you can do jumps off the ramp, skate backward, and turn without wobbling!"

When they master a skill, point out some of the advantages of the independence it gives them. "I bet you're glad you can drive now. You don't have to go around bumming rides anymore."

Once we learn to stir those dormant brain cells in children's noggins rather than sedate them with phrases that act like cerebral tranquilizer darts, those cells will begin to yawn and stretch, awakening to the real world they've been snoozing in. Over time, that yawning and stretching will turn to sit-ups and jogging, then, to strength training and iron man triathlons. Armed with brains that can think their way through any choice, simple or complex, kids will be impervious to the constant hypnotic lure of those negative peer and pop-culture influences that threaten their welfares and their futures. Once they can consciously filter all external influences, they'll be able to distinguish the true and good from the false and harmful. When all the mental racket has abated, they can listen to the quiet inner voice that day after day gains more strength. It is this strength that will equip them to make choices blind to temptation, impulse, and excuses — not just sporadically, not just for a few months or even years, but consistently for the rest of their lives.

11

WISHY-WASHY *and* CONFUSING WORDS

*a*s we have seen, phrases that tell children what to do or question their abilities hinder thinking skills. Likewise, when we communicate with them in a hesitant or ambiguous way, they have a tough time forming the straightforward internal dialogue they need to make clear and responsible choices. And when they detect a blurred border, they'll be all the more eager to cross it to get their way.

Wishy-Washy Words

One of the repercussions of abandoning the old autocratic child-rearing style for a more child-centered, democratic one has been wishy-washy parenting. Many of us were raised by strict disciplinarians who thought the best way to get kids to mind them was to *demand* obedience. For good reason, those raised this way don't look back on that aspect of our childhood with the fondest of memories. So, the last thing we want to do is treat the children we care about the same way. Recalling the harshness of our upbringing, we recoil at the thought of being a demanding boss. We'd much rather be a child's best friend than his dictator. It's no wonder that, somewhere down the line, we went to the other extreme, often using language that suggests we need to ask permission to discipline kids. God forbid we should hurt their feelings or say anything firm enough to come off as bullying. As members of the first generation that regards children as the true treasures they are, many of us have become nothing more than a bowlful of mush. But children want guides who are authoritative yet respectful, not wimpy or hesitant. They don't need another friend; they need an adult who has the resolve to guide them with a firm and loving hand. Let's take a look at some types of wimpy phrases and some suitable replacements that convey our loving authority.

Ambiguous Finishes

Not a day goes by that most of us don't finish our requests with words like "okay?" or "all right?" Sometimes we do so several times a day. I still struggle to keep myself from saying them. Here are some examples and the alternatives that will help us regain our backbone:

What to avoid:

❖ "Carry out the trash, Jimmy, okay?" Jimmy gets the impression we're asking his permission to make that request. It wouldn't surprise me if he came back with, "No, Mom. It's not okay. I'm really busy right now."

What you can say instead:

❖ Try making an impartial observation: "I see the trash hasn't been taken out yet."

❖ Try using the minimalist approach: "Jimmy, trash!"

❖ Try using humor: "Jimmy, the trash fairy is on vacation today."

❖ Follow any of the above with a limited choice, such as, "You can go out with your friends as soon as you've carried it out," or a logical consequence, like, "I've docked your allowance since I took the trash out for you when I heard the garbage truck come down the street. My time is valuable, too."

What to avoid:

❖ "I would like you to stop whining right now, all right?" Again, we're telling the little whiner to stop whining, but we're also sending him this message: "Gee, I hope you don't mind me asking you to stop, Honey. I don't want you to get upset with me."

What you can say instead:

❖ Try using an "I" message: "I really don't feel like listening to whining words. We can talk when you're ready to speak in a big-boy voice."

❖ Try providing objective information: "Whining is not allowed in our family."

❖ Try questioning: "What's our rule about whining?" (The child answers, acknowledging the family rule against whining.) "Why do we have that rule?" (The child answers, thinking about the reasons whining should not be allowed.) "Good. What do you need to do now?" (The child answers, reflecting on alternative ways of making requests and how to make amends.)

What to avoid:

❖ "Girls and boys, don't run in the halls, okay?"

What you can say instead:

❖ Try providing objective information: "Running in the halls disturbs the students in the other classrooms."

❖ Try giving a limited choice: Stop and say, "When the running stops, then we can continue on to the cafeteria to have our lunch."

❖ Stop those who are running and make an impartial observation followed by questioning: "I notice you four have either forgotten or chosen to ignore our rule not to run in the hall. Why do we have that rule in our school?" (The students answer, listing the reasons why running is against school policy.) "How could it affect others if everyone broke the rule?" (The students answer, reflecting on how rampant running could be so distracting and unsafe that learning would be difficult.) "How could it affect you if everyone broke the rule?" (The students answer, considering how these repercussions could affect each of them personally.) "What could happen to the student who ignores the rule and continues to run?" (The students answer, reflecting on the safety risks.) "Excellent. What do you need to do from now on?" (The students answer, acknowledging that in the future they need to walk in the halls.)

Pleading and Thanking

Okay, I confess. I've sometimes stooped low enough to beg my kids to behave. And I have scars from the carpet burns on my knees as living proof. The optimist deep inside me was certain they'd take pity on their poor bedraggled mom and obey my every command. I guess that inner Pollyanna was never a mother, because the pleas didn't make a dent where my kids were concerned. Nevertheless, we all have pleading in our magician's hat to get kids to behave. We say things like, "Can you please sit still?" "It would be nice if you could do what your grandfather asks," and

"Would you mind not pushing other kids in the cafeteria line?" But when we resort to reaching into the hat, children get the impression that we're close to throwing in the towel, that we can't manage them alone. Most of the time, that's true. Saying "please" or actually pleading (sometimes to the point of groveling) is often our last resort short of moving to the next state and leaving no forwarding address. Since kids are clever little things, they either take advantage of our desperation or ignore it entirely. But the truth is, saying "please" should be reserved for our personal requests, not for good behavior. On the other hand, pleading and groveling should never be a viable parenting option. Those carpet burns on our knees can really leave unsightly marks. Let's look at some examples and healthier, more effective replacements:

Instead of saying, "Please, can't you just once do as I ask and put your shoes away?"

❖ try the minimalist approach: Point to the shoes and say in an "I mean business" voice, "Ricky, shoes!"

❖ try using humor: "Ricky dear, I had no idea your shoes could sprout wings and flutter all by themselves to the closet just like a butterfly! Wonders never cease!"

❖ try logical consequences if the child habitually leaves his shoes in everyone's path, despite previous reminders or warnings: Place them in a bag and store them away. When he asks where they are, casually say, "Your shoes were out in everyone's way again, so I put them in a place where no one can trip on them and hurt themselves. When you can show me that you're more responsible about putting your belongings away, you may have them back."

❖ try providing objective information: "Shoes must go in their proper place so people won't trip over them."

Instead of saying, "It would be nice if you could stop holler-ing like that. I have a splitting headache,"

❖ try using an "I" message: "I have a terrible headache, and it gets worse with loud noises."

❖ try providing objective information and then imposing a log-ical consequence: Grasp the child by the arm, gently take her outside to the backyard, and say, "Outdoor voices are not allowed inside. You may come in when you're ready to use a quieter tone of voice."

❖ try questioning: "What's our rule about using loud voices inside?" (The child answers, acknowledging that the rule is not a figment of their imagination.) "Why do we have that rule?" (The child answers, recounting why that rule exists.) "Good. What are you going to do now?" (The child answers, reflecting on how he must be quieter when he's indoors than when he's outdoors.)

If you catch one of the kids you're chaperoning at the school dance teasing kids from a younger grade, instead of saying, "Would you mind treating those sixth graders with a little more compassion?"

❖ try giving him a limited choice: "What do you want to do, treat others nicely and stay, or call your parents to pick you up?"

❖ try making an impartial observation and providing objective information: "I noticed you were picking on those younger kids. Bullying is not the trademark of a self-confident person, and no one truly respects people who hurt others."

❖ try questioning: "How do you think those kids feel when you tease them like that?" (The boy answers, contemplating the effect his cruel words have on others.) "How do you feel when others tease you?" (The boy answers, recounting his own hurt feelings when he was teased in the past.) "What do you think is the best thing to do now?" (The boy answers, coming up with ways to take care of the other kids' feelings and to refrain from teasing in the future.)

I often overhear adults thanking children when they stop misbehaving: "Can you stop running around the store, Tom? Thank you." "Please stop pulling the cat's tail. Thank you." I even heard one child respond to his father's request that he not dawdle in the mall with, "What's the magic word?" Sure enough, the dad answered, "Please." And when the child complied, he asked his dad, "What do you say?" And the dad responded, "Thank you." Had he been my child, I would have responded to the first question with: "The magic word is NOW!" To the second question, I'd have said: "What do I say? I say good thing you're keeping up so I don't have to take you home." Here are some alternatives to thanking children for not driving you and everyone else nuts:

Instead of saying, "Can you stop running around the store, Tom? Thank you,"

❖ try using an "I" message to firmly state your expectations: "I expect you to stop running around the store."

❖ give a limited choice: "If you stop running around, we can continue shopping together. Otherwise I'm going to have to take you home."

❖ try providing objective information: "Running around the store is a good way to get lost or hurt and can also disturb the other shoppers."

> **Instead of** saying, "Please stop pulling the cat's tail. Thank you,"

❖ try allowing a natural consequence: The cat is likely to give the kid a good clawing.

❖ try using an "I" message and giving a limited choice: "I don't like seeing people hurt animals. You can either stop or get away from the cat until you can treat him nicely."

❖ try using questioning: "What's our rule about bothering Mitten?" (The child answers, acknowledging the rules regarding the handling of animals.) "What can happen to you if you keep doing it?" (The child answers, reflecting on the consequences of being rough with animals.) "How do you think Mitten feels when her tail is pulled?" (The child answers, empathizing with Mitten.) "How can you play with Mitten without being too rough?" (The child answers, coming up with healthier ways of handling Mitten.)

Sure, we can secretly be grateful they're obeying the rules, but thanks should be reserved for those times they comply with requests that don't have anything to do with getting them to behave. Kids should follow our reasonable rules because it's the right thing to do.

Apologizing for Disciplining

That adults practically ask permission to discipline kids and then apologize when they do so doesn't surprise me in the least. As I've mentioned before, the last thing most of us want is for kids to see us as bullies, tyrants, or dictators whose only purpose in life is to make them miserable. So, when we do have to lower the boom, we often get on our hands and knees to beg for their forgiveness. Here are some examples and their healthier alternatives:

Instead of saying, "I'm sorry, but you're going to have to go to time-out," when a child sasses you,

❖ just send him to time-out, period, with an explanation like this one: "Sassing is not acceptable in our family. You'll have to stay in your room until you are prepared to discuss this civilly."

❖ try giving a limited choice: "You can either behave civilly or go elsewhere until you can."

❖ try using an "I" message: "It hurts my feelings when someone treats me rudely. And when they do, the last thing I feel like doing is letting them have their way."

Instead of saying, "I'm sorry, sweetie, but I warned you that if you broke your curfew one more time, you'd be grounded,"

❖ try making an impartial observation, providing objective information, and then delivering a logical consequence: "I heard you come in past your curfew last night. In our family, kids your age must be in by ten, because it's dangerous to drive in the city past that time. You need to put your social life on hold until I feel you're responsible enough to remember and follow that rule." (See how the consequence continues until the child earns his privilege back rather than imposing it for an arbitrary time period? Make them work to regain what they lose!)

❖ try giving a limited choice: "You can either honor your curfew or give up your freedom to go out at night at all."

❖ try using an "I" message along with a logical consequence: "I worry when you come home past your curfew. I have to take away your driving privileges until you prove to me that you can abide by the rules we set."

Never feel guilty about disciplining children. In truth, you're doing them a big favor. You're enforcing the limits they need to feel secure, you're imparting important values, you're helping them grow in character, you're teaching them the importance of following rules, and you're showing them that breaking rules usually brings on unpleasant consequences. If they don't learn these lessons now, they'll learn them from a much harsher teacher — the hard, cruel world.

Negotiating

When it comes to getting kids to behave, many of us have negotiating skills so highly developed we put Colin Powell to shame. But when you think about it, negotiating is just another form of pleading in that they're both ways of asking permission to discipline. And unlike directives and commands, negotiating leads children to believe they have a say in whether to follow the rules or not. Since their attention spans are rarely longer than that of a gnat embryo, these long-winded discussions either irritate them or lure them into La-La Land, glazed eyes and all. Imagine a child enduring something like, "I know you want me to buy you that candy bar, but sweets are bad for you. Perhaps if you promise you'll be better about brushing your teeth, I might think about it. The problem is, sugar can make you so wild [this implies the chocolate, not the child, is in control of his behavior]. Do you think you could be good if you ate this much sugar? Let's see how you act during the rest of our grocery shopping." After listening to these idle promises and weak compromises, I'd be so bored that watching paint dry would seem exhilarating by comparison. Furthermore, if we conduct our negotiations under the guise that they *do* have a say in the matter, it becomes a bribe. For instance, if I said, "Tell you what, I'll let you have that candy bar if you stop your whining, promise to behave all week, and eat your vegetables at dinner every night for the next week," I'd be telling my child that I'm willing to pony up something to get him to behave. Like pleading and bribing, it sends them the message that we can't deal with them on our own and are willing to bend our rules as a last resort. However, if our rules and boundaries are clear and reasonable, following them should not constitute a negotiable matter.

Words of Surrender

There are times kids drive us to that special state of mind — a state where our facial muscles begin to twitch, bald patches appear on our scalp from pulling our hair out, and small whimpers escape our lips. It's times like these we fantasize about packing our bags and running out the front door as fast as our weary legs can carry us. And sometimes we verbalize those occasions — our way of waving the white flag, throwing in the towel, surrendering to the enemy. When children hear phrases like, "I just don't know what I'm going to do with you!" or, "Argh! I give up," they think, "Oh goody. I got the whole house to myself, 'cuz Mom's at the end of her rope. Hmm. Maybe I'll stick my froggie, Kermit, into the VCR and see if he shows up on TV. Or maybe I'll give the cat a haircut." Once they realize we can't handle them on our own, they see us as wimps who are certainly no match for any kid — even a defiant two-year-old.

There are other times when we have no intention of giving in but throw our hands up with a dramatic flair and announce our surrender just for effect. This is our way of making kids feel guilty about finally pushing us over the edge. Sometimes it works, especially if we have them programmed to feel mortified anytime our feelings are hurt or we're about to collapse into a quivering, drooling mass. But more often than not, these words just invite kids to revel in their newfound sense of power. Let's look at some examples and their healthier, more effective replacements:

Rather than saying, "I give up. I can't do anything with you!" when your daughter is caught playing hooky for the third time this year,

❖ try imposing a logical consequence by appointing a reliable peer to walk her to school and make sure she stays there until the end of the school day. You can also work with her teachers or the school principal to devise a jointly created and enforced plan. For instance, your child can be required to have her school planner or a daily attendance record signed each period and then brought home for your perusal and signature. Perhaps she can receive a detention every time she's accumulated three periods that have gone unsigned.

❖ try imposing another type of logical consequence by suspending her social privileges. You can say, "I can't allow you to be outside the house other than during school hours until I feel comfortable that I'll always know where you'll be."

❖ try providing objective information along with an "I" message, then following up with a logical consequence: "When kids skip school, there's usually a deeper problem behind it than boredom. I'm your mom. I love you. So, naturally I worry about things like drugs, academic troubles, and peers that are bad influences. Since we're a family and each of us could have contributed to this problem in some way, I've booked an appointment with a family therapist. Hopefully, she'll be able to help us sort this all out."

When your grandson has a temper tantrum in a restaurant, instead of saying, "I don't know what on earth I'm going to do with you,"

❖ try giving him a limited choice: "Either you quiet down right now or we're going to stop eating out together for a while until I think you can behave in a way that doesn't disturb us or others in the restaurant."

❖ give him a logical consequence: "I'm taking you home to your parents so I can come back and finish my meal in peace."

❖ try using an "I" message along with a logical consequence: Take him outside, find a chair or bench, and sit down with him in your lap. While you gently restrain him so he won't thrash around and hurt himself, say, "I have to stop you until you learn to stop yourself."

It might seem kids would revel in their newfound power when we throw in the towel, but deep inside, they wonder, "Am I not worth the effort?" They need stability in their lives, which means we should never give up when it comes to guiding them. When you do reach the end of your rope and run out of discipline options, tell the child, "I'm really upset right now, and I'm afraid I might say or do something I don't want to do. I'm going to take a couple of minutes to calm down and decide what I'm going to do about your behavior, but in the meantime I want you to sit quietly and stop yelling." You can also ask him to see things from your point of view for a moment: "If you were in my situation, what would you do when a kid behaved like you are now?" Kids appreciate the implication that we can actually imagine them making adult decisions. Furthermore, we seize the opportunity to evoke feelings of empathy.

Needless Explanations and Lectures

Now that the trend is toward a more democratic adult-child relationship, many of us are essentially wimpy politicians constantly lobbying for children's good behavior. It irks them to no end when we stand behind our senatorial pulpit to begin our tiresome filibusters. Do our long-winded lectures and explanations work? Take a look at Congress today and...well, need I say more?

Our explaining *why* they should behave doesn't make some lightbulb miraculously turn on in their noggins. It's not going to get them to ponder our logic for the first time with thoughts like, "Hmm. He has a valid point there. Why didn't I think of that? When he's finished here, I'm going to march right over to Mr. Johnson to apologize for cutting down his four-hundred-year-old oak tree with Dad's new chain saw." Nope. They're going to either daydream about the forty-seven other ways they can cause mischief or think about how obnoxious, know-it-all, and boring we are.

So, instead of subjecting children to tiresome speeches like, "You shouldn't curse, because it isn't gentlemanly, and it might give people the wrong idea about you. I'm sure you don't want others to think you're an uneducated, uncouth boor. If you don't clean up your language you might have a hard time selling yourself in a college admissions or a job interview. Plus, what if you have your eyes set on a girl who'd be offended by such language?"

❖ try giving him a limited choice: "Either you clean up your language or leave the room."

❖ try an "I" message: "I really get offended when I hear language like that."

❖ try providing objective information: "We don't use foul language in our family. We believe in behaving like ladies and gentlemen."

Confusing Words

Although we don't mean to, sometimes we say things to children that could be misinterpreted, are ambiguous, or leave them thinking, "Huh?" When they look at you as though you've just moved here from another galaxy and are speaking in some weird alien tongue, take that as a sign that their cerebral cogwheels are jammed. Once those wheels are locked up, kids aren't going to produce any internal dialogue clear enough to make a logical choice. Here are three ways we adults confuse children, along with the WD-40 alternatives that will keep those cogwheels turning smoothly.

Double Standards

Although kids may be works in progress, most grown-ups are too. Not many adults can say they have none of the bad habits they forbid in their children. Some habits are deeply rooted. So if we create a different set of behavioral standards for ourselves from what we impose on the children we guide, they'll have a hard time making sense of the logic behind any rule they break.

Does this mean we have to become perfect angels the moment children slither out of the birth canal? Hardly. And if any of you are models of faultless behavior, you're giving me an inferiority complex! I don't know how many times my kids have sent me to my room without supper for some of my own bad habits. In fact, I think I may still be grounded for one thing or another. I'm just clinging to the hope that they've forgotten.

Just what *can* we do to eliminate those phrases that imply a double standard? Let's look at some examples:

When your sixteen-year-old granddaughter protests after you've caught her smoking behind the house, instead of saying, "Look, I've smoked for thirty years. No way I'm quitting. But I will not tolerate the use of tobacco in my grandkids. Period,"

❖ try using an "I" message: "I know you feel I'm being unfair, but even though I smoke, I believe it's wrong. I don't want you to get hooked like I did when I was your age, because I love you and want you to stay healthy. I'll tell you what,

193

maybe you can help me quit. Let's talk about what we can do together."

❖ try providing objective information accompanied by an "I" message: "Smoking is very bad for anyone's health — kids and adults. I really want to quit this nasty habit, but until I do, I forbid you to smoke, and I'll do anything to see that you don't."

❖ try an "I" message followed by questioning: "I know I shouldn't smoke. I'm trying to quit, and I rue the day I started. Why do you suppose people begin smoking, even though they know it's bad for their health?" (The teen answers, considering the factors that lure people into this habit, including those pressures that affect her.) "How can smoking affect one's health?" (The teen answers, listing the health risks of smoking.) "Do you think most smokers are like me and wish they had never started?" (The teen answers, thinking that, despite how impulsive the choice to smoke is, the ordeal of quitting is a lengthy and arduous process.)

When you punish your daughter for cursing and she argues, "How come I can't curse? You say bad words all the time. That's not fair!" instead of saying, "Because I'm the grown-up. I can do anything I want. Besides, that's no way for a young lady to talk!"

❖ try making an impartial observation and providing objective information: "You're right. I guess I do slip from time to time. But cursing offends some people. That's impolite. So I'll do my best to stop. We'll help each other, okay?"

❖ try sharing the same consequence: "You're absolutely right. We should both stop. Why don't we fill this jar with marbles and take one out every time we say a bad word? If, by the end of the week, it's at least three-quarters full, let's have lunch together, my treat." Two-liter cola bottles should not be used in this instance.

❖ try using an "I" message: "I know I shouldn't ask you to behave a certain way while I behave in another. I don't like hearing myself use foul language. I feel ashamed when I see that it makes some of my friends feel ill at ease. From now on, I'm going to do my best to stop. Meanwhile, I forbid you to use foul language, and I expect you to stop."

One advantage of using any of these alternative approaches: if you aren't an angel already, you may soon get your wings! Sometimes I wonder if children are put on this earth to make us better people. We love them enough to break our most obstinate bad habits, because it's important to us to be the best possible role models for them. After all, they do deserve the best.

Ignoring Inner Dishonesty

All kids make excuses, rationalizations, and justifications. They go through life in and out of a state of denial, this self-deceit protecting them from the guilt and embarrassment their wrong-doings bring them. Yet we adults often look the other way, even when their inner dishonesty is so glaringly obvious it may as well be broadcast through a bullhorn. Why do we put our earplugs in so they can go on shielding themselves from the truth? Here are some of the reasons:

❖ Confronting children's inner dishonesty requires a lot of effort, especially when we know darn well that calling their bluff will result in a modern-day showdown at the OK Corral.

❖ We love them so much that we don't want to give another thought to their flaws. When they mess up, we're often just as eager as they are to justify it.

❖ Since we care about them, the last thing we want to do is hurt their feelings by pointing out their mistakes and imperfections.

❖ We engage in our own inner dishonesty from time to time, too. So, it seems as natural a human phenomenon as napping, although in this case, our inner sentry does all the napping, allowing irrational and dishonest thoughts to sneak in and influence our attitude, our choices, and our judgment.

Nevertheless, we do them an injustice when we don't draw their attention to their rationalizations and excuses. We need to call them on it when they do things like make up some lame excuse for, say, digging holes into all the chocolates to find the ones with their favorite fillings; when they rationalize their way out of keeping a promise to babysit the neighbor's kids; when they blame the dog for tracking size six, obviously human shoe prints across the living room carpet; or when they blame their teacher for a bad grade that was really a result of their not putting in enough time studying. If we let these things slide, that infamous inner dishonesty mechanism just gets stronger and stronger until, eventually, their inner sentry becomes incapable of separating truth from fiction. In short, whenever children are not being honest with themselves, we need to have the courage and patience to call their bluff. Let's look at a few examples and their unambiguous alternatives:

Instead of ignoring your child when she, face covered with chocolate, blames her pet parakeet for poking holes in all the chocolates:

❖ try using humor along with impartial observations and a logical consequence: "Darn it, I told the pet store I wanted a parakeet that wasn't a thieving chocoholic, as so many of them tend to be. But wait — you seem to have a pound and a half of chocolate on your face while Tweetie doesn't have one speck on hers. I expect you to clean up this mess right now, then get your allowance so I can take you to buy another box of chocolates to replace the ones you ruined."

❖ try providing objective information: "In our family, we admit when we've done something wrong. It's thoughtless to ruin an entire box of chocolates in search of a favorite one."

❖ try using an "I" message if she does come clean: "I admire the courage you showed in admitting what you did. That's difficult even for many adults."

Instead of ignoring your child when she blames the dog for her muddy tracks on the carpet:

❖ try using an "I" message: "I feel hurt not only when people show disrespect for my hard work keeping these carpets clean, but also when they show disrespect by not owning up to their mistake."

❖ try providing an impartial observation and objective information, and follow these up with a logical consequence: "The dog has been in the backyard all day, but I see you have mud all over your boots. It's against our rules to wear dirty or muddy shoes inside. I want you to get the steam cleaner and clean up this mud."

❖ try providing objective information followed by questioning: "In our family, we believe in being honest with ourselves and others. I see it was hard for you to admit that you made these tracks. Why is that?" (The child answers, reflecting on the reasons behind her dishonesty. This reflection also gives her an opportunity to confront and own up to any inner dishonesty.) "How do you feel when you are honest with yourself and don't use excuses or rationalizations to explain away your mistakes?" (When the child answers this question, she might realize that it's actually a relief, not a burden, to be honest with herself and others.) "What do you need to do now, both about your muddy tracks and your dishonesty?" (When the child answers this question, she'll come up with how she plans to clean up the mess, how she intends to be more honest in the future, both with others and herself, and how she plans to make amends for her muddy tracks, as well as her lies.)

Let's look at one last scenario in greater detail. Suppose your grandson Josh has been excited about the prospect of playing varsity baseball his sophomore year of high school, but he skips the second day of tryouts and comes home right after school instead. You ask him why, and his sullen retort is: "Aw, baseball is a stupid sport. Too many practices, games on the weekends — I don't have time for that anymore." You might reply with: "Last week you could hardly sleep, you were so excited about trying out for the team. I have a feeling there's something else going on. What's happened since then?"

Josh answers, "Well, maybe I'm a little disappointed. I really wanted to play first base, but that position was given to Tommy Barton already. I saw it on the results list for the first cut. I still have a chance at shortstop, though."

You might then say, "Well, you and I talked about that possibility. Didn't you say you'd be fine with that position?"

Josh: I guess. But Jonathan Tuttle did a lot better than me yesterday. What if he gets it instead? Then I have to play on the B team.

You: I see your point. I know you'd be disappointed, but then again, you know what will happen if you don't go to the tryouts at all. So what have you got to lose? The worst that could happen is you play B-string until next year. But if you give up on all your hard work this year, including those summer skills camps you went to, then you may not be playing on any team. Whatever you decide to do, I'll support your decision. If you need a ride to tryouts now, let me know.

Josh: Who am I kidding? At least I have a fighting chance of making some position on varsity. I'm good enough to be on varsity, but they'll never know if I don't prove it to them. I'd rather play baseball on the C team than not play at all! Thanks for offering me a ride, Grandpa. Hang on, and I'll get my stuff.

You: It took a lot of courage to admit your feelings to me and to yourself. It's hard to face a difficult situation, but as you're saying, you miss so many opportunities when you hide from them. I'll be waiting for you in the car.

Once children realize you won't let them pull the wool over their own eyes any more than you'll let them pull it over yours, they'll understand the healing power of the truth. Being honest with others can be very refreshing. But being honest with ourselves — whether we're children or adults — can produce a profound inner clarity that keeps our decisions faithful to the truth and bolsters our self-esteem.

Unreasonable Rules and Boundaries

Although at times it seems to take forever, children do grow up. So, it's not much of a stretch to see that the rules and boundaries we set for them must be tweaked from time to time. For instance, you can't expect a fifteen-year-old to reasonably accept having the same boundaries appropriate for an eight-year-old imposed on her. She'd probably give you an earful if her bedtime remained fixed at seven o'clock for all those years! And she'd probably go ballistic if her curfew was forever etched in stone: "Be in by dusk, or you're grounded."

Clearly, we can't keep children in padded cells under our constant supervision until the tantrums and then the hormone surges have abated and they've made it into adulthood. This might seem easier than letting them live their lives, but if we want kids to become self-directed, we must instead provide them with clear guidelines and rules to live within. They need to learn to behave within these guidelines because it's the right thing to do, not just because they don't want to get in trouble. When rules and boundaries are unreasonable, they lack logic. And without logic, confusion takes root. Once children are confused, they can't use sound reasoning skills to make choices that are under their complete and conscious control. This ambiguity will probably not facilitate healthy internal dialogue that says things like, "I need to be home by 9:30 P.M. because after that there might be a lot of drunk drivers on the road. Anyway, I need time to finish my homework and get enough sleep to wake up early for school in the morning." Instead, the thinking they're likely to engage in will revolve around how unreasonable their parents are — as in, "What does he think I am, a two-year-old?" — or it will be externally directed — as in, "I don't know why he's trying to ruin my life, but if I don't do what he says, he's going to take the car away again. I'm just going to have to find a way to either catch him off-guard by asking him to extend my curfew when he's not paying attention, or break it behind his back and hope he doesn't find out." Not exactly the focus we intend them to have.

To make sure your expectations change appropriately as children grow up, explain the importance and rationale for each rule and periodically review the rules together. If they're old enough, you can ask them for their input, but only if you can be open to any suggestions they make. Remember, though, when in doubt, trust *your* intuition over *their* begging and whining. The following are some examples of unreasonable rules and boundaries and their reasonable counterparts:

Instead of saying, "I don't care if you're sixteen; you're too young to date,"

❖ try offering a reasonable compromise: "I think I'd feel comfortable if you started out with double dating. If you and your friend Tracy make that sort of arrangement, you two can help watch out for each other."

❖ try questioning, but mostly for the purpose of hearing their side. Questions that might help you understand their logic might include: "Why do you think our rule against dating before you're seventeen is unreasonable?" "Is there any way you can make sure I'm comfortable about you going out with someone I don't know well?" or, "Can you devise a plan so that if things go sour on the date, you can contact me to pick you up?"

Instead of saying, "Under no circumstances can you grow your hair out. No son of mine is going to look like a hippie,"

❖ consider whether this is a battle worth fighting. After all, what's the worst that can happen if your son has long hair? Are you concerned about how it would reflect on you as a parent? Are you concerned that he'll be judged unfairly? Although standards for what's acceptable vary according to many things, including cultural background, race, religion, and geographical region, we must look past our fixed ideas to objectively assess whether our rule does more harm than good.

❖ try sharing your concerns using "I" messages: "I know a lot of your friends are growing out their hair, but my concern is that you'll be judged unfairly by others. For instance, in a job interview, your potential employer might equate long hair with lax morals or a poor sense of responsibility and work ethic. That means, as unfair as it may seem, he might choose a less qualified, short-haired applicant over you. I just want you to take that into consideration before making your decision."

By eliminating unreasonable limits and double standards and therefore exposing and forbidding children's inner dishonesty, we remove the ambiguity that undermines the adult-child relationship. Free from this ambiguity, children have no reason to focus their attention in counterproductive ways. They aren't given the easy way out of difficult situations, such as relying on excuses, self-deceit, or rationalizations to make their wrongdoings more palatable. Instead, we give them the logic they need to develop a keen understanding of every ingredient crucial to making a responsible choice — a choice based on their true sense of right and wrong rather than what short-term advantages they stand to gain.

12

WORDS THAT ENCOURAGE EXTERNAL DIRECTION

*i*t takes time for children to develop an inner compass strong enough to guide them consistently. Until then, they *will* make mistakes. They *will* get into trouble. They *will*, during the most inconvenient moments, drive us bananas. And since desperate times call for desperate measures, some adults will opt for a short-cut to good behavior in children by either dangling carrots in front of their noses or a sword of Damocles over their heads. But when we rob kids of the consequences they should experience for their poor choices by using bribes, rewards, threats, Santa Claus, and other external influences to make them obey, we, their guides, also rob them of valuable learning opportunities — opportunities that only come from adult-child dialogue and the lessons learned from consequence. Lessons like these are what help children become adults who can weather any temptation or challenge when making their choices — adults who are whole beings with sound judgment and inner strength. That said, we must remove all external beacons as strategies to encourage obedience in children. Only then can their inner compass develop into a reliable tool for guiding them through the peer, media, and pop-culture jungle unscathed. With that tool, children will become self-directed rather than externally directed. Let's examine some of the external beacons we use and some healthier alternatives.

Bribes and Rewards

We've all used bribes and rewards — the counterparts of those evil twins threats and ultimatums — and I'm no exception. We pull out that ol' bag o' bribes in an attempt to magically transform unruly barbarians into willing and obedient children. Parents and grandparents use rewards, for example, to get children to stop wetting their beds, do their chores, and make better grades. Teachers and other adults taking care of children shower them with stickers, stars, or enviable titles as rewards. We offer them bribes to stave off potentially embarrassing public tantrums, to get them to fetch our newspaper, and to circumvent any fusses at the pediatrician's office. Setting up little contests between siblings to get them to obey, a tactic we'll discuss later, is also a type of bribe. Why do we resort to them? Because they work really well, doggone it! For me, learning to refrain from bribing my kids was like parting ways with a trusted ally.

Unfortunately, these devices aren't effective in getting children to comply with our wishes for the right reasons. The more we use rewards and bribes, the more children rely on them for motivation. In his book *Punished by Rewards,* Dr. Alfie Kohn claims that children who respond to rewards aren't behaving themselves; the rewards are behaving them. He goes on to write that although rewards can motivate children, they only motivate them to get the reward, while intrinsic motivation suffers as a result.* Anything they see as a

---

* Alfie Kohn, *Punished by Rewards* (Boston: Houghton-Mifflin, 1993), page 26.

prerequisite to something they covet appears less desirable to them because they sense a loss of control and autonomy. For instance, if a child is told he'll get a lollipop if he helps set the table, he sees the chore as something that stands in the way of him getting that lollipop. Having to set the table becomes a drudgery, a tether that keeps him from his prize. But if that child were to see setting the table as a way for a small person to truly contribute something meaningful to "big people," then he's in charge of the chore, not vice versa. Or if he sees setting the table as something new that he's only seen big people do, the prospect of taking on the task may excite him. Lollipops and other bribes take the excitement and intrinsic motivation out of every task.

Children then become less interested in meeting a challenge for the sake of meeting a challenge, as rewards and bribes encourage them to perceive that challenge merely as something standing between them and their prize. Whatever obstacle we ask them to overcome in order to get their prize is therefore undertaken with less determination and commitment. They therefore focus only on the destination and miss the journey entirely. They learn to obey the rules others make for them just because they're rules, and they'll be rewarded if they follow them. This means they do not fully grasp lessons and integrate them into their value system, and therefore they never develop true character. Furthermore, when we offer children rewards (or praise for that matter), we don't bother figuring out the reasons for their misbehavior, whether it's misbehavior that's actually happening or misbehavior we're trying to preempt.

As children learn to expect goodies for every good deed they perform and every time they don't misbehave, they hone their skills of manipulation to work this to their best advantage. Power struggles often result, while the bribes and rewards reinforce their sense of entitlement. For example, when my children were young, I didn't travel much, but when I did, I made the regrettable mistake of telling them, "If you mind the babysitter, I'll bring you back a little treat." I'd come home missing them so much I could hardly stand it. If you've traveled in the past as well, you may have seen me. I was the crazy woman on the plane who sobbed over her kids' photos in her wallet. But the moment I got home, dropped my bags, gave them a hug, and asked, "How are you?" they'd spit forth, "Fine, whaddya get me? whaddya get me? whaddya get me?" It made me feel like running back out into the street, flagging down my cab, and booking it back to the airport, but, being the inexperienced mother that I was and still being so happy to see them even though they were far more interested in their presents than me, I did the second worst thing: I launched into a martyrdom speech that would have made Joan of Arc feel second rate: "I go away for four days and miss you terribly, and all you care about is what I brought back for you..." This went on for at least fifteen minutes before I stomped off to my room to unpack my bags.

When kids see life as a road paved with bribes and rewards, we end up having to compensate them for everything we want them to do, even if just to behave civilly. In other words, they learn to be guided by external, rather than internal, beacons. So what happens when those external beacons aren't around? What happens when they go out into the real world, where bosses don't reward you for showing up for work on time and policemen don't bribe you to obey the speed limit? What happens when they come to realize this, and their own inner compass is undeveloped? We can't hover around them for the rest of their lives, continually dangling carrots in front of their noses. Frankly, I want my children to behave in the checkout line because they don't want to disturb others, not because they want a box of Gobstoppers. I want them to get good grades as a reflection of their enthusiasm for learning and their willingness to work hard, not because they'll get a bigger allowance. I want my children to stop peeing in their Pull-Ups because they don't like wearing something cold, wet, and stinky, not because Grandma promised to take them out for ice cream if they stay dry. Let's take a peek at a few examples of bribes and rewards and replace them with healthier phrases:

Instead of saying, "Be a nice girl, Rachel, and stop crying. Grandma promises to buy you a candy bar when we check out if you do,"

* ❖ try giving a limited choice: "You can either settle down or we can go home and Grandma can finish shopping on her own."

* ❖ try imposing a logical consequence: Leave your shopping cart behind, take her by the arm, and, without saying a word, drive her to a friend's or neighbor's house so you can return to finish your shopping. It's a good idea to set up co-op agreements with other adults so they can extend the favor and you can reciprocate.

* ❖ try providing objective information: "It disturbs others to hear that kind of noise."

Instead of saying, "Wow, you made all A's on your report card. Go get my wallet, because it has a twenty-dollar bill with your name on it!"

* ❖ try making an impartial observation: "By the looks of these grades, you seem to have really developed strong study habits."

* ❖ try using healthy praise: "You must feel proud of this accomplishment. It shows a lot of dedication and enthusiasm for learning."

* ❖ try questioning: "How do you feel about your accomplishment in school?" (The child answers, reflecting on the inner pride

that accomplishment created.) "What do you think you did to earn these good marks?" (The child answers, contemplating the effort, perseverance, and enthusiasm that it took to succeed.) "How do you think ongoing academic success might affect your future?" (When the child answers this question, he might reflect on how this will improve his chances of getting accepted into the college of his choice, expand his base of knowledge to one that serves him well throughout his life, enhance his sense of self-worth, open up more career choices, and strengthen those character traits required for such success.)

Instead of saying, "If you guys agree not to fight in the car on our way to Astroworld, I'll let each of you buy a souvenir there,"

❖ try giving a limited choice: "If you don't fight in the car, then I won't be so distracted on the highway that I have to turn back."

❖ try imposing a logical consequence: Drive them back home at the first sign of a skirmish. You can use the same explanation about your being distracted in order to construct the logic.

❖ try providing objective information and giving an "I" message: "It is unsafe for me to drive when there are loud noises in the car. I have a hard time concentrating on my driving. I might have to turn back and go home."

Say you're a nurse in a pediatrician's office wrangling with two toddlers who are using the exam table as a trampoline, digging through the trash can (ugh), and tossing tongue depressors at each other. Their mother is in the corner trying to read a 1979 issue of *Ladies' Home Journal.* However, her parental overload fuse has clearly blown, causing one corner of her mouth to twitch at regular intervals. Instead of saying, "You boys be nice, and I'll give you a balloon,"

❖ try using humor: "Calling all circus animals! Let's line up for the weigh-in before the next act. Everybody follow me to the scales. Hup, two, three, four, hup, two, three, four…"

❖ try the minimalist approach: Whisper what you want them to do as if it's classified information. Toddlers love secrets. They'll probably come close, cup an ear, and place it as close to your lips as they can, then giggle expectantly, excited to be the only ones in the world partaking in this covert operation.

Now when my children utter those four little words I've come to despise, "What do I get?" I simply say, "You get the satisfaction of a job well done," or, "It isn't your birthday already, is it?" or, "Whatever you can afford, dear." Works like a charm.

Invoking a Higher Authority

Although invoking a higher authority could be considered a threat or an ultimatum, I address this common strategy here because it, too, encourages external over internal thinking. Though the most ubiquitous example is surely invoking the authority of the other parent ("Just wait until your father gets home," or "I wouldn't want to be you when your mother sees the mess you've made"), there are vast possibilities for the types of authorities we can invoke and where and when it's tempting to do so. Other adults besides parents defer to this tactic too, such as grandparents ("Don't make me get your parents on the phone"), teachers ("Do you want me to send you to the principal?"), and camp counselors ("Lights out, or the three-toed maniac will come and eat you"). At restaurants and other public places, we can invoke those who work there ("Sit down at the table now, or I'll have to call the manager over.") Another popular one is invoking the police, which is often useful in the car ("Look! There's a police car behind us. You'd better buckle your seat belt fast!"). We can invoke anonymous authorities ("You better not do that, because you might get caught"), and we can call on imaginary villains as a scare tactic to get kids to obey us ("Go to bed before the boogeyman gets you," or, "The purple people-eater eats children who don't finish their veggies"). During the holiday season we have my personal favorite, the trump card of calling on Santa Claus to keep children from turning into wild animals ("I'd hate to have to call Santa Claus right now"). I've been known to stage phony phone calls to the North Pole to verify, in front of my kids, that Santa's naughty and nice list hadn't been finalized yet.

We use these sorts of phrases because they work. However, when we invoke these higher authorities, kids respond because they're afraid of what will happen to them if they don't, not because whatever they're doing is wrong. But, every time we invoke a higher authority, we tell children we can't manage them on our own. And they grow up believing the reasons for behaving appropriately rest solely on the shoulders of the outside world, not on theirs. They don't stop to consider their actions based on real consequences, so their inner compass remains undeveloped, while their reliance on excuses and rationalizations proliferates like bunnies in the spring. Here are healthier ways of expressing some of these examples:

Instead of saying, "Look! There's a police car behind us. You'd better buckle your seat belt fast!"

❖ try giving a limited choice: "If everyone gets their seat belts on, then we can go on to the store like we wanted."

❖ try providing objective information, using an "I" message, and giving a logical consequence: "It's not safe to drive without seat belts. I don't feel comfortable taking any risks by driving without them fastened. We'll have to try our little outing at a later date. Everyone out of the car."

❖ try using the minimalist approach: "Seat belts, everyone."

Instead of saying, "I'd hate to have to call Santa Claus right now" when your daughter refuses to go to bed,

❖ try making an impartial observation and then providing objective information: "I see you're not in bed, and it's a school night. Kids who don't get enough sleep are usually not able to do their best in school the next day."

❖ try questioning: "What's our bedtime rule?" (The child answers, reviewing the rule.) "Why do we have that rule?" (The child answers, acknowledging the rationale behind the rule.) "What can happen if you don't get enough sleep?" (The child answers, reflecting on the purpose of the rule.) "What do you need to do now?" (The child answers, conceding that she must respect her set bedtime.)

❖ try having her experience a natural consequence by letting her feel sleepy the next day. Be sure you follow this up with dialogue so she can turn that consequence into a lesson: "You seem very tired today. Do you have any idea why?" (The child answers, reflecting on the repercussions of going to bed too late.) "Kids need at least nine hours of sleep a night. What time do you need to get to bed to make sure you get nine hours?" (The child answers, calculating the hour by which she must go to bed to meet those sleep requirements.)

Instead of saying, "Sit down at the table now, or I'll have to call the manager over" while you're at a restaurant,

❖ try imposing a logical consequence by dropping the child off at a friend's house or with a babysitter, then returning to finish your meal. If that's inconvenient, have your child apologize to the neighboring tables or the manager of the restaurant. It may embarrass her, but at least she learns how she must behave to avoid feeling that way.

❖ try providing objective information: "The people in the restaurant can't fully enjoy their meals when they see little kids running around the place."

❖ try giving a limited choice: "You can either sit quietly at the table or I'll assume you're finished eating and will have the waiter remove your plate." If she's already finished, you can rephrase this: "If you can sit quietly at the table, then I won't have to take you home now."

Instead of saying, "Don't make me get your parents on the phone" when your grandkids sass you,

❖ try giving them a logical consequence: "I won't allow people to talk to me disrespectfully. I want you to leave the room until you are willing to discuss this politely."

❖ try the minimalist approach: Give your grandchildren a stern look and say their names firmly.

❖ try providing objective information: "The only discussions that get anywhere are ones in which everyone is treated respectfully."

Instead of saying, "Do you want me to send you to the principal?" when a student uses foul language,

❖ try giving a limited choice: "You can either clean up your language or sit in the hallway until you're ready to."

❖ try providing objective information followed by a logical consequence: "Foul language offends others. You need to wait
outside in the hall until you are ready to speak civilly. Then, I
expect you to apologize to your classmates."

❖ try questioning: "What's the rule about saying bad words in
class?" (The student answers, acknowledging the rule's existence.) "Why is it important to follow that rule?" (The student
answers, reflecting on how cursing offends some people and
can affect one's reputation adversely.) "What do you intend to
do the next time you feel the urge to use foul language?" (The
student answers, reflecting on self-monitoring and self-talk
strategies that might help him use other, healthier forms of
communication.) "How do you plan on making amends to
those you offended?" (The student answers, recognizing the
appropriateness of apologizing to those he has insulted.)

Instead of saying, "Lights out, or the three-toed maniac will
come and eat you,"

❖ try giving a logical consequence: Go to the cabin, unscrew the
lightbulb, and take it with you.

❖ try providing objective information: "The only ones who can
go canoeing tomorrow are the campers who get a full eight
hours of sleep. The others will have to stay behind with the
assistant counselor until we return."

❖ try using an "I" message: "It's hard for me to sleep when you
campers are so noisy. If I'm not well rested, I'm cranky and
uncooperative the next morning."

Using "Other People"

We don't always look only to Santa, the chief of police, or the
boogeyman to get children to obey. Sometimes, we include all or

part of the entire human population to achieve the same effect, as the following phrases clearly illustrate: "What are other people going to think when you act like that?" "Those people at the next table are looking at you. Maybe you'd better settle down," or, "I hope nobody sees you bringing your drink into the theater." No wonder children grow up thinking they're on stage in front of an invisible audience that inspects their every split end, mole, freckle, and mistake. Here are some better alternatives:

Instead of saying, "What are other people going to think when you act like that?"

❖ try giving a limited choice: "If you settle down, we'll be able to stay and watch the show."

❖ try using the minimalist approach: Give the child a stern expression and say his or her name in a firm and serious tone.

❖ try providing objective information: "Others can't enjoy the show when they're being distracted by a lot of noise."

Instead of saying, "Those people at the next table are looking at you. Maybe you'd better settle down,"

❖ try making an impartial observation, followed by objective information: "The people around us seem to be bothered by your behavior. Whether or not they are, banging on the table and blowing bubbles in the glass of water is behavior that is distracting and disruptive and therefore not appropriate."

❖ try imposing a logical consequence by canceling your plans to have dessert afterward with, "Since you can't seem to control your behavior in this restaurant, we're going to have to go home as soon as we've paid the check rather than stay for dessert." You can also insist he apologize to the manager and those he disturbed.

❖ try providing objective information: "Noisy behavior isn't allowed here."

Instead of saying, "I hope nobody sees you bringing your drink into the theater,"

❖ try providing objective information: "They don't allow people to bring drinks into the theater unless they've been purchased here."

❖ try giving a limited choice: "When you finish your drink, then we can go into the theater."

❖ try making an impartial observation: "It looks like they don't allow people to bring in drinks that have been bought somewhere else."

Blame-Shifting

Children who are uncomfortable with their own mistakes and failures treat them like hot potatoes — they can't get rid of them fast enough. So, they shift the blame to someone else. For instance, one day I came home from work to be greeted by cake batter all over the kitchen cabinets. Against my better judgment, I gazed upward and saw dollops of dough suspended precariously from the ceiling. Now, I don't mind my kids honing their chef's skills, but not without my permission and not if it involves a messy food fight. Before I could open my mouth, I heard, "I couldn't help it. I tripped!" "It's not my fault. It was Erik's idea!" "Michelle told me it was okay with you," and, "The dog made me do it." When my kids pull a snow job on me, I make sure they all know they alone are responsible for the choices they make. Even though temptations lure them into trouble, the ultimate decision is theirs. How did I respond (after I had caught my breath, that is)? I said, "Nice try, kiddos. But tripping over your own two feet couldn't have caused this mess. Heck, a full-blown seizure couldn't. And though it may have been Erik's idea, I'm sure he didn't threaten you with death by spatula. Michelle may have misspoken for me, but deep inside, you know I wouldn't have allowed you to fling dough from pillar to post. And, last but not least, Zoe doesn't have an opposable thumb. She can't *make* you do anything, unless licking you to death is enough of a threat. I want this mess cleaned up within twenty minutes, or I won't be able to trust any of you in the kitchen for quite some time." By the way, the cake was delicious, but I don't *even* want to guess what extra ingredients went into the batter to spice it up.

Even though kids are naturals when it comes to escaping accountability, sometimes we actually encourage them to shift the blame for their mistakes. I've heard adults say things like, "I don't want you to hang out with Alex. He gets you into too much trouble," "Look what he made you do!" and, "It's not your fault. Your parents just didn't raise you right." (Yep, I've actually heard grandparents use this one!) When we say things that encourage kids to shift all or part of the blame for their choices, it's like telling them their decisions are not under their own control, but that external forces, like poor parenting, bad genes, negative peer associations, and bad luck, are the culprits instead. How can we reword these phrases so that children can accept full responsibility for their actions?

Instead of saying, "I don't want you to hang out with Alex. He gets you into too much trouble,"

❖ try giving a logical consequence followed by an impartial observation: "I can't let you hang out with Alex anymore. You don't seem to make good decisions when you're with him." By rewording it this way, you let the child know that although outside influences can make it more difficult for him to choose wisely, the choice still belongs to him.

❖ try giving a limited choice: "You can hang out with Alex again once you've shown me that you can control and be accountable for your choices and not allow peers to influence you negatively."

❖ try providing objective information: "Each of us is responsible for what we do, regardless of the influences we encounter."

Instead of saying, "Look what he made you do!"

❖ try providing objective information: "No one can make a person do anything. Our decisions are always ours, and ours alone."

❖ try using humor: Tickle the child while saying, "Oh, I see. So he tickled you like this until you surrendered and did what he told you to do? That rat!"

❖ try questioning: "Was it okay to do what he told you to, even though you knew it was wrong?" (The child answers, reflecting on how his choices should be based on right or wrong rather than someone else's advice, instructions, or directives.) "Who's responsible for what you did, you or Reggie?" (When the child answers this question, he confronts whether or not he is truly in control of his choices. He also reflects on the fact that, regardless of outside influence, he and he alone is responsible for every choice he makes.) "What do you need to do next time Reggie tells you to do something you know is wrong?" (The child answers, listing strategies for resisting peer pressure and asserting his right to make his own choices.)

Instead of saying, "It's not your fault. Your parents smoke like chimneys," when your grandson tries to finger his parents' bad influence after you catch him smoking cigarettes in your garage,

❖ try offering objective information: "Everyone is responsible for their own actions, good or bad. I know your Mom and Dad both smoke, but in our family, we don't believe in blaming our poor choices on someone else's."

❖ try using an "I" message and giving him a limited choice: "I expect you to own up to your mistakes. You can either discuss this with me honestly, or I can take you home to your parents and we can all discuss this together."

❖ try using impartial information, offering objective information, and delivering a logical consequence: "I see you're uncomfortable taking ownership for your mistakes. Nevertheless, we are all in complete control of what we decide, even if that choice is to take on someone else's unhealthy habits. Pack your things. I'm going to have to take you home to your parents so you can let them know what has happened. We all have your best interests at heart, and we want to help you make healthy choices in life."

Let's look at one more example. Say your daughter does poorly on her social studies exam, and you comment, "You usually enjoy that subject. Did the test cover something you didn't quite understand?"

She responds with, "It's not my fault. It's that cow of a teacher, Ms. Myrtleson. She always puts things on the tests that aren't on her review sheets. How fair is that?"

You counter with, "You and Suzy talked for hours on the phone last night. Do you think that might have cut into your study time?" The conversation then continues as follows:

Your daughter: I dunno. Maybe. But that teacher is still evil. She hates me; I just know it.

You: What could you have done to prepare for those questions that weren't on the review sheet?

Your daughter: Nothing, except move to a different school. It's hopeless.

You: Was all the material covered in the textbook?

Your daughter: I guess. But I didn't know that. So, I didn't bring it home.

You: I can imagine how upset you are, because you seem to take great pride on how well you prepare for these sorts of tests. What could you do differently next time?

Your daughter: I guess I could ask the teacher to explain exactly what's going to be covered. That might help the rest of the class, too. And I could go to the after-school tutorials she has the day before each test.

You: Hey, that's not a bad idea! Do you think Suzy might be your study buddy on those nights?

Your daughter: Yeah, she's good at helping me focus, and she's a whiz at organizing notes from the textbook. I'll ask her to help me prepare for the makeup test Thursday.

You: Sounds like a good plan.

Once children believe outside influences determine the choices they make, they tend to repeat the same mistakes. After all, how could they feel responsible for something they can't fully control? And how can they stop from repeating a poor choice if they never feel a sense of ownership and responsibility for the first one?

There are other phrases that tell children their mistakes come from outside sources and therefore encourage them to strengthen their reliance on external beacons. For example, "What made you do that?" or, "What brought all this crying on?" Be sure your wording makes it clear that the child is responsible not only for his choices, but also for the consequences they produce, good or bad. Replace blame-shifting phrases with ones that reinforce full accountability; for example, "Why did you decide to do that?" or, "Why are you crying?" Such a subtle difference can make a big impact on whether children own up to and therefore take control of their behavior.

Giving Children Second (or Third or Fourth) Chances

Time and time again, we act as parole officers for children, letting them off the hook by overturning whatever sentences we've levied for their misbehavior. Why? Being the ex-champion of second chances, I can list a number of reasons for this form of leniency. For one, sometimes I find it too inconvenient to follow through. For instance, say I'm at the movies with my kids when one of them starts making rude noises with their mouth. I might tell them I'm going to take them all home, fully intending to do just that, but after thinking about how I'd have to put up with the protests from my other kids, stand in line to get a refund for the tickets, and come up with some other way to entertain the whole rowdy bunch — well, it just doesn't seem worth it. (Besides, I didn't want to miss one single second of *Finding Nemo*.) So, as my kids could probably have predicted down to the last syllable, I'd utter my well-practiced, "Okay, I'll give you one more chance. But I better not hear another peep." There are also times we threaten kids with punishments we have no intention of carrying out, but more about this later.

Another reason we give children second chances: we feel sorry for them. We can't bear the thought of them staying home with a sitter while the other siblings take off for the amusement park. We can't sit by and watch them suffer in time-out. We can't deny them the toy we promised them.

Sometimes, we cave in because we don't want them to hate us. And other times, we actually just forget about the punishment altogether. I've done this before. In fact, I remember once asking one of my smaller kids why he didn't go to time-out when I asked him to. He said, "Because I was waiting for you to forget." Those kids know me all too well. In fact, children make serious business of knowing how adults tick so they can use that information to their best advantage.

But when we give children a way out, we imply we don't have faith in them to overcome an obstacle, endure suffering, learn from a mistake, or handle a consequence — a negative message to send, especially to children, credulous things that they are. Furthermore, when we let them off the hook again and again, they learn to base their decisions to behave or misbehave on the likelihood of getting another chance. Again, they look to external rather than internal cues to make their decisions. In the end, we're rewarded with a pattern of poor choices and poor behavior. Now that's *really* inconvenient!

Instead of letting them off the hook with, "Okay, fine. I'll give you just one more chance. But if you blow it, you're in serious trouble!" be sure you stick with whatever consequence you imposed to begin with. Once kids know we mean what we say, they stop trying to manipulate us into repealing the consequences we deliver, and they understand that we are their disciplinarians and their guides, not their court of appeals. Let's look at some phrases that give children a chance to escape the consequences they've earned and some that don't:

Instead of saying, "Okay, if you promise to be good from now on, you don't have to go to time-out,"

❖ try giving a limited choice: "If you go to time-out now as you're supposed to, I won't have to add extra minutes."

❖ try providing objective information: "In our family, we have certain standards of behavior that we all must follow. When we don't, we must experience a consequence, and there are no exceptions to that rule."

❖ try using an "I" message: "I don't change the rules I make. As hard as it may be for you, I have faith in you to accept your time-out and reflect on how you'll make better choices in the future."

Instead of saying, "Fine, even though you didn't wash the dishes beforehand like I asked, you can go to Johnny's birthday party. But this is the last time I'm going to let you off the hook!"

❖ try providing objective information followed by questioning: "In life, we have firm consequences for our poor choices. What do you think our world would be like if criminals were able to talk their way out of their sentences?" (The child answers, reflecting on the fact that consequences for wrong-doing can encourage us to make better decisions in the future.) "Knowing that I do not give second chances, what do you need to do now?" (The child accepts the fact that you aren't backing down on this or future disciplinary decisions and acquiesces to washing the dishes.)

❖ try offering objective information: "In our family, we have faith in each other to make responsible choices from the start or to accept the consequences if we don't."

❖ try giving a limited choice: "You'll be late, but when you've finished washing the dishes like you're supposed to, I'll give you a ride to Johnny's party.

Idle Threats

Who hasn't been so tired at the end of the day that settling down with a cold beer and the remote sounds a lot more appealing than managing a household of hellions and somehow getting them to wind down for the night? At times like this, we often delude ourselves into believing that idle threats will be enough to bring peace and order to our surroundings. Well, I've got news for you: they're not. I was once an armchair disciplinarian myself, and I resorted to all sorts of idle threats, but the most I ever got out of them were great thigh muscles. "Don't make me get out of this chair," or my all-time favorite, "Don't make Mommy tell you twice!" would send them scurrying for a few seconds, but as soon as I settled back into my La-Z-Boy, they'd return to their mischievous ways. So I'd have to raise myself a few inches from the chair and glare until they started scrambling for cover again. Back and forth we'd go until my leg muscles burned with lactic acid buildup and my kids grinned from ear to ear.

It isn't just parents who try idle threats with children. Teachers shout out, "You'd better quit pulling Michelle's pigtails, or I'm sending you straight to the principal." Although usually notorious for creating a punishment-free zone for their grandkids, grandparents might say, "If you don't stop unraveling my favorite quilt, Bobby, I'm going to wring your scrawny little neck." (Fathers seem to be fond of this one, too.)

As much as I appreciate having buff quadriceps, I now realize that idle threats can cause a lot of harm. Kids who are subjected to them begin to ask themselves, "Is this the time it matters to be good or not?" And they seek answers to such questions in external signs like our energy level and facial expression. Kids are pros at distinguishing an idle threat from the real thing, so if we don't truly mean business, their usual conclusion is, "That grown-up's not going to follow through. There's no time like the present to get away with murder."

There are ways to forgo idle threats and make all our lives easier — even children's. Unfortunately, the only casualty might be those quads and hamstrings, but there's always Thighmaster for those. Let's look at some alternatives:

Instead of saying, "Don't make me get out of this chair," when little Dean starts to paint the kitchen walls with chocolate pudding,

❖ try giving a limited choice: "Either you put the pudding back in the fridge or you will not be allowed to have any for dessert for the rest of the week."

❖ try providing objective information: "This pudding is for eating, not painting."

❖ try using an "I" message and imposing a logical consequence: "It annoys me when someone messes up my nice clean walls. I want this cleaned up right now."

Instead of saying, "Don't make Mommy tell you twice!" when Christina refuses to peel herself away from the television set to do her chores,

❖ try imposing a logical consequence by removing her TV privileges for a day.

❖ try making an impartial observation: "I see you've been watching TV past our family's limit and your chores are still not done."

❖ try using the minimalist approach: "Christina, chores!"

Instead of saying, "You'd better quit pulling Michelle's pigtails, or I'm sending you straight to the principal,"

❖ heck, send the kid without another thought!

❖ try giving a limited choice: "You can either stop pulling Michelle's pigtails, or I can move your desk to the front row."

Mischievous kids don't take a shine to this maneuver — too much exposure.

❖ try questioning: "Why do we have rules against teasing or hurting another classmate? (The child answers, recognizing that there is indeed such a rule and reflecting on why it exists.) "How do you think Michelle would feel if your behavior went unpunished?" (When the child answers this question, he recognizes that Michelle would want her feelings acknowledged, not dismissed.) "What do you need to do to take care of her feelings?" (The child answers, coming up with a way to make amends.) "Now that you know such behavior always has a consequence, what do you need to do right away?" (The child answers, accepting his imminent rendezvous with the principal.)

Instead of saying, "If you don't stop unraveling my favorite quilt, Bobby, I'm going to wring your scrawny little neck,"

❖ try the minimalist approach: Say his name, and when you have his attention, waggle your index finger to indicate you want him to stop.

❖ if he's small, simply put the quilt where he can't get his restless little fingers on it.

❖ try providing objective information and using an "I" message: "That quilt was made by hand by my great-great-grandmother. It means a lot to me, and I am hoping to pass it down to you one day, if it's still in one piece."

Having come to the end of this chapter, you probably have a perplexed, if not a poleaxed, expression on your face and are wondering, "Now what the heck am I supposed to do? This lady just took away all my best ammo!" Although these time-honored strategies stand a good chance of getting children to behave, the compliance is almost always temporary. Instead of contemplating the consequences and solutions for their poor choices and coming up with healthier alternatives and ways to avoid repeating the same mistake, kids are going to be engrossed in how angry they are with us, how inadequate they feel, how they can worm out of a punishment, how they can be sneakier next time, or how they can take revenge. This all contributes to tarnishing our relationships with them.

When we replace the phrases in this chapter with ones that encourage children to rely on their inner compass for guidance, they learn to do the right thing — not out of fear of our reaction or a reliance on some other external influence, but because it honors the value system we've helped them integrate into their moral fabric. This is so important it bears repeating: as they grow up, those unfiltered external influences won't be limited to Santa Claus, star stickers, lollipops, and their parents' approval; they'll include the whims of their peers, popular culture, and the media — forces unlikely to have children's best interests at heart. Furthermore, taking such shortcuts to make kids more manageable does not achieve any meaningful or sustainable good; it's like taking a shortcut through the jungle to avoid a band of hyenas only to be swallowed up by a massive pit of quicksand.

13

WORDS *from* SIBLINGS *and* PEERS

$n$ow we know what *we,* the adults who care for children, must change. But what about other kids? After all, they can influence children, too. Siblings, classmates, complete strangers we may never meet — can't they inflict just as much harm in the way they communicate with children? Sticks and stones may break their bones, but, let me tell you, words from other kids can leave some nasty bumps and bruises too.

Sibling relationships, in particular, can be the most influential and enduring in a child's life. Our job is to help ensure that influence is positive, that they learn and grow from it rather than regress and feel bitter and small.

The truth is, we can't protect kids from everyone and everything. We can steel them against harm to the greatest extent humanly possible by encouraging self-direction and modeling clear communication; once we do this:

❖ they won't see others as keys to acceptance,

❖ they won't view others as potential adversaries against whom they must compete for that acceptance, and

❖ they'll be able to effectively handle those who mistreat them.

Freeing them from the first of these — needing acceptance from other kids, whether siblings or peers — is the foundation we will have built by changing our own communication style with them. Now let's explore the second and third attributes listed above — avoiding seeing others as potential adversaries and handling mistreatment from others.

Discouraging Sibling and Peer Rivalry

Nothing irks adults more than the inevitable squabbling between kids. "Why can't they just get along?" we ask. The battles are usually noisy, include a tear or two, maybe a fistful of hair, bald patches, scratches (especially if girls are involved), and a few bruises that they milk for months even though they don't give a second thought to those they accumulate after a weekend of skateboarding. On top of that, nobody wins these skirmishes. They just give up, exhausted, until the bell for the next round dings.

But the fights children have are a necessary part of growing up. If we try to squelch them completely by forbidding their disagreements, they never learn to resolve interpersonal conflicts constructively and amicably. They never learn how to compromise, negotiate, or just "agree to disagree." Childhood is the training ground for this, and in families who forbid conflict, siblings often grow up to be emotionally distant and unaffectionate with one another — plus, they never master the art of getting along with those with whom they don't see eye to eye. That said, although we don't want to force kids to stay out of the boxing ring, there are things we can do to make sure what they learn will enrich their relationships with each other and everyone else who crosses their paths in life. As you will see, some of those things involve breaking old habits, while others relate to lessons we can pass along.

Avoiding Contests

Few things get children to behave well or comply with our requests better than taking advantage of their competitive spirit. One of the most popular ways of doing this is setting up little contests between them. When my children were very young, my husband would turn them into his personal lackeys just by looking at his watch and saying excitedly, "Let's see how many seconds it takes you to get the newspaper," or, "I bet you can't get me a drink of water in forty seconds or less! Hurry up. I'm timing you. On your mark, get set, GO!" By the time they reached the age of ten or so, they had wised up; the only responses he could eke out of them were exasperated groans, rolling their eyes to the back of their head with the finesse only an adolescent can manage, and that "Yeah, right" look that means: "I'm on to your gimmicks, man."

I, on the other hand, would set up contests to pit one sibling against the other so that they'd do what they were supposed to do. One of my most timeworn phrases: "Let's see who can get dressed for school the quickest!" (I like to look on the bright side, though: if they ever drop out of college, they can always nab jobs as quick-change artists in a vaudeville act.) From time to time, though, that little trick of mine would backfire, launching one kid toward the other's jugular with fangs and claws bared and ready for action. What's worse, when kids are preoccupied with snatching at each other's throats or inflicting some other form of bodily harm on one another, the last thing they're thinking about doing is getting ready for school. So, what can we say instead that will encourage children to lend us a hand when we ask them to and make them focus on doing what needs to be done without maiming their sibling competitors?

Instead of saying, "Let's see who can get dressed for school the quickest!"

❖ try making an impartial observation: "I see it's almost time for the school bus to come, and neither of you have gotten dressed yet."

❖ try the minimalist approach: "Boys, your clothes!" or point to the clock and say, "Boys, the time!"

❖ try allowing them to experience a natural consequence: Let them miss the bus, then say, "I'm sorry you guys didn't get ready in time for school. I guess this means you'll have to walk. You might be late, but at least it's nice weather."

If you're a teacher, instead of using the time-honored "I like the *waaayy* Sarah is sitting so nicely" to get other kids to stop jumping up and down like a troop of monkeys on a banana plantation,

❖ try the minimalist approach: Continue teaching, but lower your voice to a whisper.

❖ try giving a logical consequence: Stop the lesson, sit down at your desk, and read a book. Chances are, the class will be curious enough about your reaction that they'll calm down. Then you can give them a limited choice: "If you're ready to sit still and listen, then we can continue the lesson."

❖ try appealing to their desire to contribute. I can explain this best with a personal anecdote: Over the years, I've substituted for kindergarten teachers on many occasions. (Before I get to the point, let me just say that by the time the bell rang at the end of the day, I could just kiss the ground those permanent teachers walk on.) After my first couple of stints as amateur teacher, I discovered that it's not easy to contain and focus an entire roomful of child-generated enthusiasm. If we could harness it, it would mean the end to the world's energy concerns. I clearly remember a fine spring day a few years back when the class I was teaching was exceptionally rambunctious. One child in particular seemed to be spurring everyone else into a state of gleeful frenzy and silliness. I decided that if I stood any hope of maintaining my sanity, I had to solve the problem through him rather than try to get each student to settle down. Instead of focusing on what he was doing to contribute to the anarchy, I placed *him* in charge of solving it by pulling him aside and saying, "Damian, I need your help getting this class under control. They seem to listen to you. Would you please think of some signal that will remind them to settle down?" Since every child hungers for some way to contribute to the group, especially when that contribution is genuinely needed, Damian suddenly transformed before my very eyes. The expression on his face changed from his usual Dennis the Menace mischievous grin to a solemn look of self-importance rivaling that of any world leader's. From his new position of authority, Damian announced to his fellow kindergarteners that whenever he held up three fingers, they were to be quiet. When things got anywhere close to rowdy, up flew those fingers like a drum major's baton. This was serious business for the guy. And as a man on a mission, he remained calm and collected the rest of the day.

Instead of saying, "Let's see how many seconds it takes you to get the newspaper,"

❖ try a simple request: "Jimmy, would you mind getting the newspaper for me?"

❖ if he whines and balks, offer objective information: "We believe in helping one another in our family," or, "Whining and complaining are irritating and are not allowed here."

❖ if he refuses, you can also try "I" messages: "It hurts my feelings when you're not willing to help me out."

Instead of saying, "I bet you can't get me a drink of water in forty seconds or less! Hurry up. I'm timing you. On your mark, get set, GO!"

❖ try making a polite request: "I'm so thirsty. Would you mind getting me a drink of water while you're downstairs in the kitchen, Courtney?"

❖ if she protests, try an "I" message: "I'm really beat after working all day. It would really mean a lot to me if you did that small favor when you get a chance."

❖ try giving her a limited choice along with an "I" message for acknowledgment: "Could you please get me a glass of water? You can either get it now or you can wait until the next commercial comes on. I would really appreciate it."

On the subject of requests, when it comes to encouraging kids to lend us a hand, getting rid of contests is a good start, but it's not enough. It's also important to phrase those requests politely and only make them when the kids themselves are not swamped or exhausted. As tempting as it may be to turn them into little slaves, we need to be reasonable. For instance, just because they're smaller and younger, I wouldn't ask my children to fetch me a blanket while I'm reading a book if they're up to their eyeballs in homework. So, first ask yourself, "Would I make that same request of an adult?" If the answer is "yes," go for it. If not, do it yourself! You might also ask, "How would I feel if someone asked me to do the same thing?" If you'd find it insulting, then it would be unreasonable to expect a child to feel differently when presented with the same request.

In short, setting up contests for any reason is a no-no. Those contests that pit child against child or child against the clock encourage children to see other kids as potential adversaries they have to beat, and winning as a prerequisite for acceptance. This only fans the fires of a winner/loser attitude. Aside from sporting events, the only contests in which we want children to participate are those where they compete with themselves rather than with one another. Those contests that urge them to do our bidding are merely ways of exploiting them for our personal gain. When we use these to our advantage, we show a lack of respect and a presumptuous superiority. However, when we eliminate contests from our bag of tricks, children have one less external influence dictating their behavior — one less puppet string making them dance to our tune. For every such string that's cut, children are freer to make their own moves, to dance their own dance, to chart their own course — all traits of the self-directed.

Minimizing Sibling Rivalry

The driving force behind most sibling squabbles is the struggle to compete for parental love and approval. And when children vie for attention within the family, they embroil any adults within shouting range into what can become an intense power play that has been known to bring grown men to their knees, begging for the torture to come to a swift and merciful end. When children pit parent against sibling to exact revenge on that sibling or to seek a larger share of parental love and attention, their conflict is not a fertile field for personal growth and stronger bonds; it's a battlefield strewn with resentment and jealousy. Here are some suggestions that can minimize the rivalry and make conflicts between children productive, enlightening, and thus worthwhile.

Don't Interfere

Never interfere with sibling arguments unless death and dismemberment are distinct possibilities. Naturally, it strikes fear in any sane adult to see kids tussling in a ball of dust, hair, and limbs, but in truth, children seldom hurt each other badly. The only time I stick my nose in my kids' business is when their fights disturb my peace, whereupon I take them each gently by the arm, toss them out into the backyard, and, in my most pleasant voice, tell them, "You may come back in when you've worked things out." Of course, the first couple of times I did this, I had to scramble like a bronco out of a rodeo chute to lock every door to the house. When they tried to fool me into believing they had reached a truce, it would sometimes take all of my sleuthing powers to uncover their ruse. (Usually, the exchange of evil glares with one another was enough to tip me off.) If the truce was a sham, the fighting usually resumed within three seconds after they crossed the threshold, whereupon I'd calmly toss them out again, this time for much, much longer. (I find these moments perfect for that long-awaited bubble bath.)

Don't Get Sucked In

Never let them pull you into their disputes. When one child says something like, "Kristina said I was a stupid dork," reply with, "You didn't believe her, did you?" If they whine, "Annika hit me!" you might say, "I have faith in you two to work it out on your own," or, "Hmm. You two were getting along so well yesterday. I wonder what's different today? Whatever it is, I'm sure you'll figure out a way to solve it." You can also provide objective information like, "In our family, we take care of our differences on our own." At first, kids will continue to protest with, "But Mom..." If they do, simply restate your case without taking anyone's side, pointing fingers, criticizing, and so on. For instance, say, "I'm sorry you two are unhappy with each other. Nevertheless, it's not my job to settle your arguments. That's something you can handle on your own." You can make it even simpler by saying, "Not my job!" every time they squeal.

No Tattling

Tattling comes as naturally to children as breathing. However, my position is to never allow tattling in the family unless someone is in danger of getting seriously injured or if someone's property is poised in front of a proverbial wrecking ball. If one of my children tries to tattle about some egregious injustice a sibling inflicted on him or her, I'll respond with, "We don't tattle in our family except to prevent someone from doing something dangerous or from breaking something. Unless that's the case, this is a job you can handle on your own." Sure, they protest and roll their eyes with as much drama as they can muster, but over time, they stop coming to me with constant reports on the questionable doings of their brothers and sisters that make them sound like a sports commentator at a soccer match. I guess the message has sunk in, because I can't remember the last time I overheard one of my kids say, "Oooo, you're busted! I'm telling Mom!"

Don't Take Sides

Be sure to acknowledge children's feelings without taking sides. For instance, if the child comes crying to you about the incisor marks embellishing him thanks to his big brother, instead of saying,

"I know how you feel. I hate when your brother acts like that," you can say something like, "I'm sorry you're hurt, but I know you can handle him on your own." I only deliver logical consequences to the perpetrator when I witness the offense myself. That way, I'm acting on firsthand information rather than hearsay, therefore minimizing the chance that the victim will suffer his sibling's vengeful wrath.

Don't Label

Never label one sibling in front of the other or compare one to another — either positively or negatively. When a child is told she's tidier than her sibling, the messier one is going to make life miserable for the other. And when a child has his nose rubbed into his brother's better grades, he might find ways to take revenge on that brother. As far as labeling goes, whether Brent hears you call Cameron a "boy genius" or a "clumsy oaf," those monikers are going to be powerful ammo for future sibling wars.

Don't Play Favorites

Never play favorites. Many adults have stronger connections with one kid than another. If that's the case with you, keep your preferences under wraps. Kids pick up on the subtlest of signals, and if they get wind of your preferences, they'll compete even more intensely for your love and approval. Sibling rivalry will hit unprecedented levels, the power struggles will intensify, and self-esteem will be the first casualty.

Make Children Feel Special

Kids want to feel they have a unique and personal relationship with you, so make each child feel special. I use one-on-one time to share the long list of things I think are so special about each of my children. Nighttime is perfect for this, because you've got a captive audience; tucked into their beds, they're not going to dash off to another adventure. Their minds are still, and you're snuggling with them — what better time to talk about how much you love them?

I also have what we fondly refer to as "Buddy Day." Each of my five children has his or her own special day of the week, when we spend one-on-one time together, and nothing takes priority over that time. We've even made up secret handshakes and sayings to go along with it. Our outings are usually something brief: going out for ice cream, having a Slurpee at Target, or going to the neighborhood park to ride on the merry-go-round and swing on the swings. One thing I forbid, however, is using that time to buy them things, like toys or clothes. Buddy Day is about enjoying time together, not getting something. For several years now, each of my kids has looked forward to their special Buddy Day with Mom, and I've grown to look forward to that special time with them, too.

Don't Dismiss Feelings

Never dismiss or refute children's feelings during a sibling quarrel by saying something like, "Don't be silly! You don't hate Brianna!" Instead, try acknowledging the child who feels hurt with, "I know how much it hurts you when you don't get along. I bet you two will work things out soon."

Use Impartial Observations

When kids do get along, point it out by making an impartial observation and following up with questioning: "You two are big buddies now! Do you have more fun when you get along?"

Show Children the Positive Side of Disagreeing

Discuss the advantages of constructive sibling disagreements — how they help them learn to resolve interpersonal conflicts, explore their own beliefs, test their ideas, and define their identities.

Share Your Own Stories

Share your own sibling war stories if you have any. If you're close to your brothers and sisters, let your kids know how those relationships were strengthened by working through your differences as children and adolescents. If you're not very close, talk about any regrets you might have and what you think you could have done differently.

Encouraging Love and Forgiveness

Most kids would rather be staked to an anthill with honey rubbed all over their naked bodies than be forced to either hug or apologize to another kid — especially, God forbid, a sibling. I'm not sure why we adults try to force them to offer a hug or an apology. Maybe we think they'll be magically overcome with love or remorse. Maybe we think it's an ancient custom for becoming lifelong blood brothers. But, no matter what ideas we've come up with, they're just delusions. The hugs are disguised attempts at a stranglehold or limp adaptations of a coma. The apologies are uttered through gritted teeth and stares that promise a painful revenge in the dead of night when the other least expects it. Attempting to force children to show love or remorse should, therefore, be forever nixed.

Love, compassion, and respect between kids should be allowed to develop on their own with only a slight nudge from time to time. We can accomplish much of this by minimizing rivalry and competition, as we have already discussed. And through the changes we make in our adult-child communication, we can also see to it that children grow up in a harmonious environment where everyone is allowed to have their own opinions and ideas, where everyone is comfortable *earning* acceptance rather than pursuing it out of a desperate need, and where children enjoy each other's approval but don't *need* it to be fulfilled and happy. With this foundation of acceptance, inner strength, and harmony, we can then encourage children to experiment with affection, to have the courage to reach beyond their inhibitions and fears of being in a vulnerable position emotionally.

I've encouraged this sort of experiment a number of times with my own kids — with great success, I might add. For instance, one day, when my son, Lukas, was eight and my daughter, Michelle, fourteen, they had an argument that practically rattled the pots and pans from their place in the cupboard and dislodged the caulking between the bathroom tiles. In the end, they both stormed to their own bedrooms in tears. After about fifteen minutes (when the plaster and dust had settled), I called Lukas into another room and said, "I know you don't want to fight with Michelle. You guys seem to have so much fun when you get along. Would you be open to conducting a little experiment in human behavior?" Loving science as he does — as evidenced by the recent metamorphosis of my kitchen into a look-alike for *Dexter's Laboratory* — Lukas agreed.

So, I asked him to knock on Michelle's door. Fortunately, I had coached him to ask, "May I please come in, Michelle?" in his sweetest prepubescent voice in response to her screaming out, "What do you want?!" When she said, "Okay, fine. Come in then, you creep!" he went in. (She was really curious at this point and was probably hoping he'd beg for forgiveness or promise to be her personal slave for life.) Then he went over to her, gave her a hug, said, "I'm sorry we're not getting along," and left without another word.

His not sticking around had two purposes: First, it's always good to flee the scene in case the whole thing misfires. Second, by leaving, Lukas kept it simple. If he had lingered, Michelle may have wondered if he had some ulterior motive, like wanting to play Zelda with her on her Playstation, borrowing some of her CDs, and so on. By reaching out and then withdrawing, he was proving to her that all he wanted was for things to be okay between them, and that now the next move was hers. Sure enough, after a few minutes, she came out of her dragon's lair, threw her arms around him, told him she loved him, and took him by the hand to her room so they could play Zelda together. Afterward, we discussed how the recent chain of events was proof that kindness is so powerful it can change someone's attitude from seething to melting in a matter of seconds.

You can also encourage kids to be good role models with each other, especially the older ones. Give them certain responsibilities like reading bedtime stories to the younger ones, supervising them during play, helping them with their schoolwork, and so on.

Try to enlist kids in responsibilities and activities they can do cooperatively: "Can you two help cook dinner while I bathe the baby?" or, "Maybe you both can wash the dishes while I finish the laundry."

Seize every opportunity to evoke their feelings of empathy for other children, such as, "Tommy just got scratched by the neighbor's cat. Can you do me a favor and get it cleaned up while I call the doctor to schedule an appointment for a tetanus shot?"

Children will soon learn that many friendships come and go, particularly in childhood. Kids have arguments and break up, they move away, and so forth. Use these trying times to discuss how their relationship with their siblings is a lifelong friendship they can always count on, especially if they work hard to nurture it.

To cultivate closeness between siblings, have them sleep in the same room at night; when they're younger, have them sleep in the same bed (exceptions: cover hogs, snorers, and bed wetters). When children don't have an ounce of energy left to wrangle, they can quietly reminisce, share dreams, and revel in "the giggles."

Teaching Children How to Resolve
Conflicts Peacefully

When you change the way you communicate with children, several things happen. First, all environments where this communication occurs will be more tranquil. Since your language doesn't foster unhealthy competition or approval seeking, the children with whom you interact won't be scrambling for your attention, trying to knock others out of the pecking order along the way. There will be no manipulative attempts to pit you against another child, no sense that one child is better than another, et cetera. Second, you'll model a constructive expression of emotions for them. Third, you'll show children you have faith in them to resolve most of their problems on their own, and this includes interpersonal conflicts with other kids. When they understand that you have no intention of rushing in to rescue them from those conflicts, they're not going to be as likely to pick fights to begin with.

Once you establish a peaceful milieu, all that's left is for them to hone their communication skills whenever the opportunity arises. Here are some examples of how to pass that peace pipe along:

When children use any of the harmful phrases mentioned in this book, model a healthier alternative, a phrase they should be saying instead. For instance, if a boy tells his classmate, "Stop hogging the computer," say aloud, "I need time to finish typing up my report. Could I please use the computer now?" When a brother tells his sister, "You stepped on my model airplane and broke it! I hate you, you clumsy oaf!" say, "You broke my airplane, Eliza. Whenever someone breaks somebody else's stuff, it's their responsibility to replace it." After you've modeled a constructive alternative, don't insist they repeat it. All you want to do at this point is just bait the hook and hope for a nibble. If they don't bite now and rephrase their remark, it's not important. Eventually, they'll internalize what you've repeatedly modeled. When a logical consequence is appropriate, as in the second example, it will be your job to see that it's delivered and carried through. If the fighting escalates, give both parties a consequence (have them go elsewhere, forbid them from playing together for awhile, et cetera) and use one of the other tactics we've discussed throughout the book — providing objective information, giving limited choices, and so on.

I introduced a four-step approach in chapter 2 for expressing our own anger constructively. You can also teach children to follow these steps when they have disagreements with others. You'll have to guide them through the process the first several times, and they may be so angry with one another that you have to coerce them into following the procedure by, for example, giving them a limited choice, as in, "You guys can go back outside to play with the rest of the kids as soon as you've settled your argument. Until then, you'll have to sit here on the sofa." But, eventually, they'll be able to go through this process with little or no help. Again, here are the four steps:

1. Have one child tell the other that he or she is angry.

2. Have them explain why, based on the two root emotions, hurt or fear.

3. Encourage the child to state his or her expectations for the other.

4. Finally, have the child insist on an acknowledgment from the other.

If both kids are responsible for the conflict, which is almost always the case, have the other one go through these same four steps too. Make sure they both know that neither of them can speak until the other has completed all the steps. Here's an example of how two children might settle their conflict in this way:

Josh: I'm really mad at you because you called me an idiot. That hurt my feelings. [The root emotion behind Josh's anger is hurt.] I want you to stop calling me names. Okay?

Bill: Okay, fine. [Now it's Bill's turn. Make sure he doesn't begin with the word "but," because this is a qualifier that essentially refutes his promise.] I called you that because you tripped me, and I fell and dropped my whole tray of lunch on the floor. That made me angry, because not only did I hurt my wrist, but everyone laughed at me. I'm afraid people are going to think I'm a loser. [Bill's anger is based on both hurt and fear.] I want you to stop trying to trip me when I'm walking back from the lunch line. Can you agree to that?

Josh: Sure, I guess. I'm sorry I tripped you, Bill.

Believe it or not, after you've guided them through this a few times, children will spontaneously start to resolve all their conflicts using this approach. They may not do so perfectly at first, but once they see how effective this technique is, they'll prefer it to bruises and tears any day of the week.

When children are overwhelmed with anger, frustration, or some other negative emotion, you can help temper those feelings by mirroring their emotions, but to a greater extreme. Let's look at an example first, then I'll explain how it works:

Child: I'm never speaking to Cindy again! She picked Alex and Janie first for the kickball team. Some friend she is!

You: What? I thought you were her best friend? That makes me so mad I can't see straight! Maybe she shouldn't be the captain of the team! I mean, what kind of loyalty is that?!

Child: Yeah, I know!

You: If I were you I wouldn't have any more to do with her. She's acting like a traitor!

Child (in a less angry voice): Well, after all, her job as captain is to choose the best players first. I'm disappointed she didn't choose me first, but at least I wasn't chosen last! That'd be really embarrassing.

You: Hey, you're one of the best! I've seen you play! What a double-crosser!

Child (even more calmly): I know, but Alex is a faster runner and Janie can kick farther than me. I guess I would have made the same choice.

You: Yeah, but the least she could have done is warn you and give you an explanation first so you could be prepared.

Child (calmly): True, but she did come over and apologize to me when she saw how upset I was.

You: Well, all right. I guess she did the right thing after all. I shouldn't be so upset with her.

Child: Yeah, I mean she's not a bad person. She's my very best friend in the world. Can she sleep over this weekend?

You: Sure, why not?

As you can see, the child was brought back to center in response to the adult's exaggerated reaction. This works well with adults and children alike, because people generally shy away from extremes. When a person goes off the deep end, others will do anything they can to drag that person back to a more moderate position. And, as in the above example, this often requires them to rethink their own.

When children learn to treat their siblings and peers with respect and kindness; when they learn to assert themselves without making matters worse; when they learn to resolve their differences peacefully; when they learn to value each other; and when they learn that loving one another is a gift, not a weakness that leaves them vulnerable, they truly possess the most powerful ability of all: the ability to make and keep bonds with others that will add meaning, depth, and pleasure to their lives. After all, giving and receiving love is the Holy Grail of life, isn't it?

CONCLUSION

*S*o where do we begin in bringing about more effective communication with children? After all, we've discussed so many phrases we all say regularly, sometimes several times a day. Can we abandon them all overnight? And what happens if we slip? Take heart, because you really don't have to change your entire vocabulary in one fell swoop. Start, instead, by following a simple two-week exercise, outlined below:

1. Eliminate all directives (telling children what to do).

2. Eliminate negative phrases (those containing "no," "can't," "quit," "stop," or "don't") whenever possible.

3. Impose logical and natural consequences as the main form of discipline.

Whether you're a parent, teacher, adult sibling, grandparent, or another adult who interacts a great deal with kids, within that two-week period, you will notice the attitude of the children you guide (and even your own attitude) change for the better in the following ways:

❖ Your relationship with children will have less hostility and conflict. Emotional upheavals and power struggles become history, so relationships will become more fulfilling personally.

❖ If you're a parent or grandparent, the family environment will be more loving and peaceful. If you're a teacher, your classroom will stand a good chance of being nominated for the Nobel Peace Prize. If you're an adult taking care of kids, you may very well be shipped off to the Middle East to have a crack at things.

❖ Kids feel better when they're guided rather than bossed around or managed. They want to be encouraged to stick to their limits and follow rules. They also want closer relationships with adults, ones built on mutual respect that offer them plenty of opportunities to contribute something meaningful.

❖ Through this new adult-child communication, you'll begin to view children in a more positive light. You'll see them in terms of their strengths, not their weaknesses. You'll see them for what they're doing right, not what they're doing wrong. You'll see their ever-diminishing misbehavior as a golden opportunity for growth, not a scourge on your life or a criminal future for theirs. With this different perception and your newfound faith, hope and optimism abound.

❖ When kids become self-directed, they enjoy self-confidence, high self-esteem, strong character, and the tools and courage to make the right choices for the right reasons, even when doing so requires self-sacrifice, dealing with adversity, and unpleasantness. There is nothing more liberating than freeing oneself from the need for outside approval. There is nothing more rewarding than gaining acceptance through contribution rather than conformity. And there's nothing more powerful than having full command of one's own choices, and therefore one's life.

❖ It feels so refreshing to have faith in children and to watch while they prove themselves worthy of that faith over and over again. Furthermore, it's so much easier to delegate more of the responsibility to *them* for growing up well. Most of the suggestions in this book entail eliminating what doesn't work, changing to simpler approaches that extinguish misbehavior permanently, or standing by while children learn from their mistakes. So, life with children becomes a joy, not a burden.

❖ Changing the way you communicate with children in an effort to have them grow up to be self-directed rather than externally directed brings a growing awareness of the difference between the two — first in their behavior, then in the behavior of others, and finally in your own thoughts and actions. Over time, you may find yourself becoming more and more self-directed as well.

It's a good idea to read through this book every few months or so until you've successfully implemented the suggestions within it and mastered adult-child communication that encourages self- rather than external-direction. No one will snicker if you enter "Reread *Hearing Is Believing*" into your day planner or electronic organizer as a recurring event — if you deal with children on a daily basis, whether they're your own or someone else's, you have every right to rely on an external brain. I know I do!

The following are two questions adults ask me when I speak to audiences throughout the country:

❖ "Do I have to be perfect?" I certainly hope not, because I'm nowhere close. There are days I want to shield my kids from the public eye, lest there be a stampede of my readers to the refund counter. Fortunately for us, when children are guided with words that encourage self-direction, they regard the old way of communication as flawed. So when we mess up and fall back on old habits, rather than take it to heart, they just think of it as something we need to work on.

❖ "Is it ever too late?" Thankfully, no. I've seen profound results in all age groups of children, my own and others. In fact, I encourage you to apply these communication techniques to adults as well: your spouse, coworkers, employees, friends, and even complete strangers. You will see their attitudes and your relationship with them change for the better too.

If all these reasons still aren't enough to convince you to change the way you speak to children, consider this: by encouraging self-direction in kids, we become part of something very special — a movement that may change the moral landscape of our society. With the love we have for children, we have a unique opportunity before us to make real and lasting change. Imagine a world of children who grow up to be *truly* responsible, not only for themselves, but also the world they live in. Imagine a world of children who grow up to be moral, self-confident, self-reliant, accountable, compassionate, and happy. Imagine a world where all those troubles that spring from external direction either lessen or disappear altogether. Imagine this world, and you see a world children truly deserve.

INDEX

ABOUT
the AUTHOR

*E*lisa Medhus, M.D., is a veteran physician who built and operated a successful private medical practice in Houston, Texas, for thirteen years. She is also the mother of five children, ages nine through nineteen, some of whom have special challenges like Tourette's syndrome, attention deficit disorder, learning differences, and obsessive-compulsive disorder. With nineteen years' experience parenting her own children, several years' experience home-schooling her children, and thirteen years' experience as a family physician, Dr. Medhus is uniquely qualified to address the concerns of parents.

Raising Children Who Think for Themselves, Dr. Medhus's first book, has earned numerous prestigious awards including the Parent's Choice Award, the National Parenting Center Award, and the National Parenting Publications Award. Her second book, *Raising Everyday Heroes: Parenting Children to Be Self-Reliant,* offers a witty guide to help parents stop the trend of "rescuing" and start giving their children the tools to succeed on their own.

In high demand as a keynote speaker and a guest on television and radio shows, Dr. Medhus regularly discusses the issues and problems facing today's families. To learn more about her work or her speaking schedule, check her website at www.drmedhus.com.

New World Library is dedicated to
publishing books and audio products
that inspire and challenge us to improve
the quality of our lives and our world.

Our products are available
in bookstores everywhere.
For our catalog, please contact:

New World Library
14 Pamaron Way
Novato, California 94949

Phone: (415) 884-2100 or (800) 972-6657
Catalog requests: Ext. 50
Orders: Ext. 52
Fax: (415) 884-2199

E-mail: escort@newworldlibrary.com
Website: www.newworldlibrary.com